PRETTY LACE

SUSAN BATES, INC.

First published, 1986, in the United States by Susan Bates, Inc.
212 Middlesex Avenue, Chester, Conn. 06412

ISBN: 0-87040-646-9

10 9 8 7 6 5 4 3

Printed and bound in Japan

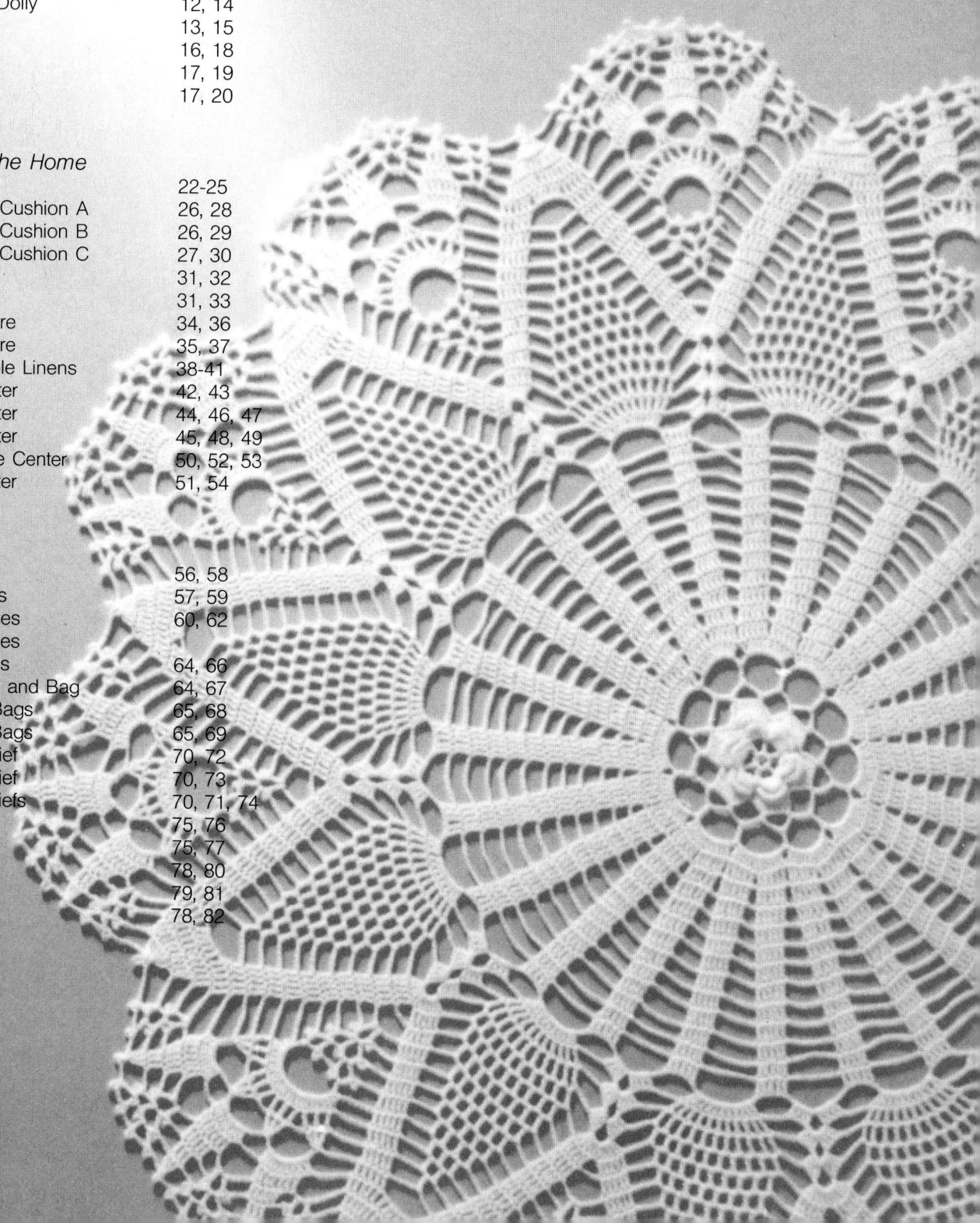

Contents

1 Doily

Materials: Anchor Mercer-Crochet no. 30 white, 20 g
Steel crochet hook no. 8 (size 0.9 mm)
Finished Size: 27 cm (11″) in diameter

Directions: Ch 6, join with sl st to form ring.
Row 1: Ch 3, dc 17 in ring.
Row 2–25: Work following chart.

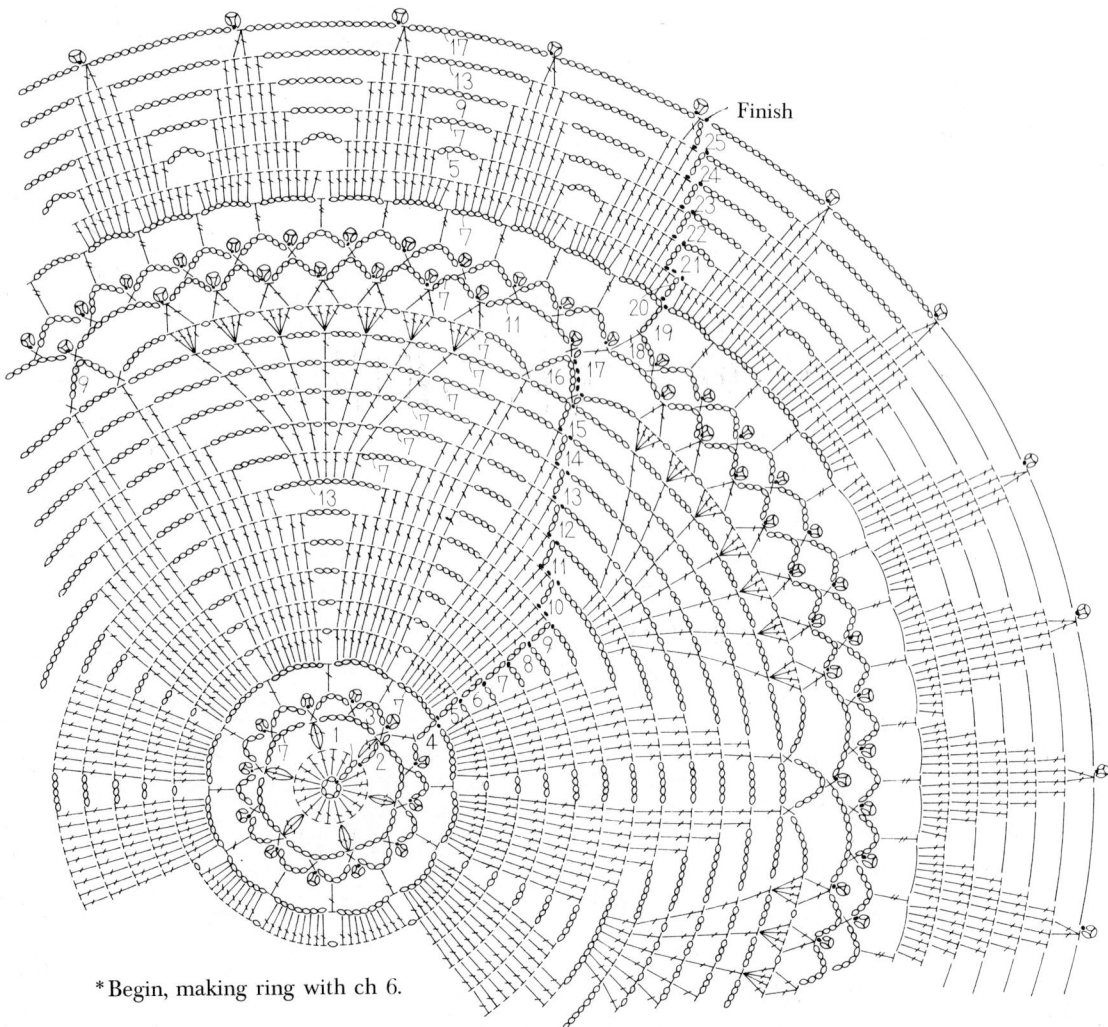

Finish

*Begin, making ring with ch 6.

2 Doily

Materials: Anchor Mercer-Crochet no. 30 white, 20 g
Steel crochet hook no. 8 (size 0.9 mm)
Finished Size: 29 cm (12") in diameter
Directions: Ch 4, join with sl st to form ring.
Row 1: Ch 4, trc 1, "ch 3, 2-trc puff" 7 times in ring; dc 1 at top of first trc.
Row 2–18: Work following chart.

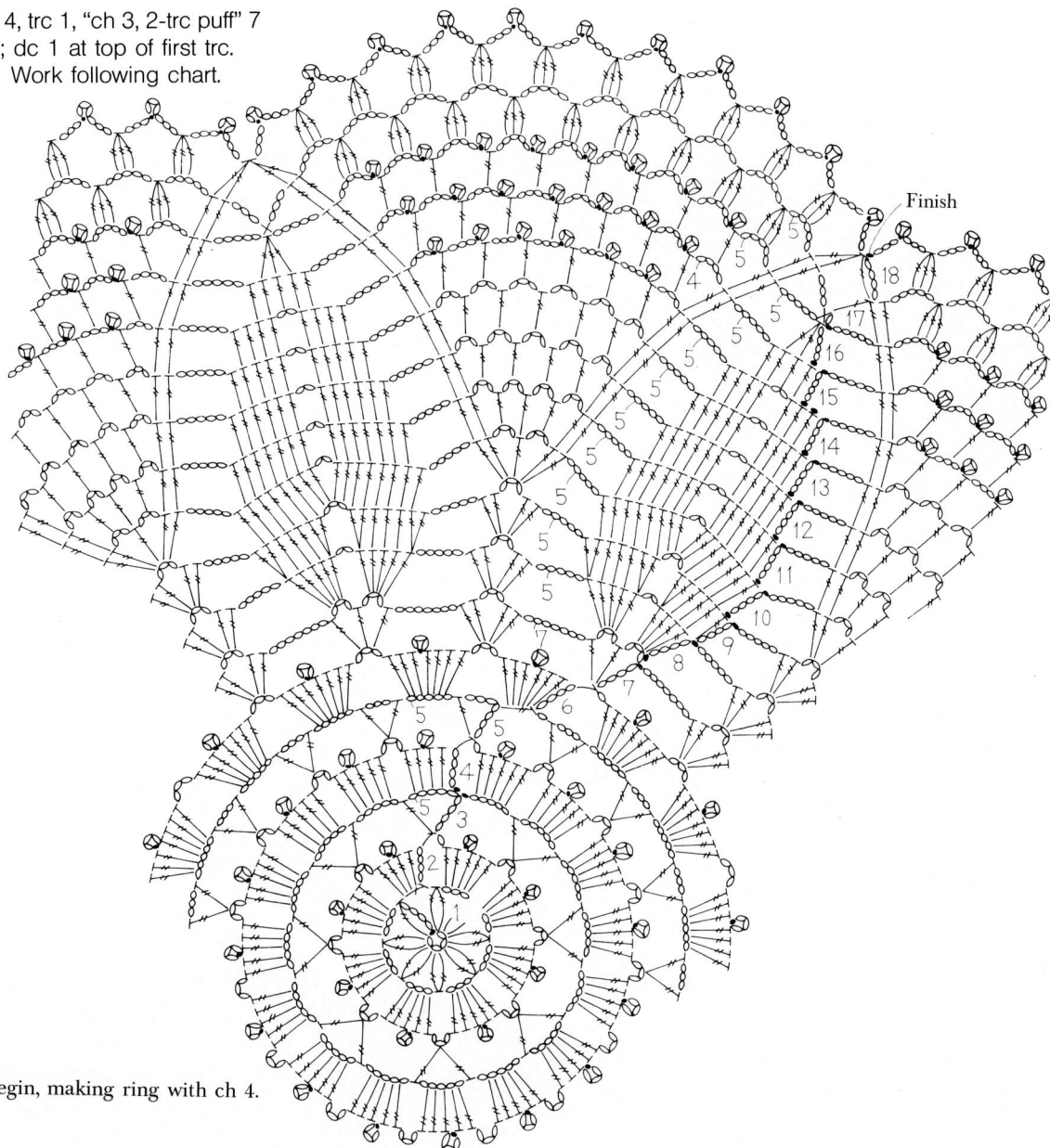

Finish

*Begin, making ring with ch 4.

3 Oval Doily

Materials: Anchor Mercer-Crochet no. 30 white, 20 g
Steel crochet hook no. 8 (size 0.9 mm)
Finished Size: 20.5 × 35 cm (8 × 14″)
Directions: Work in numerical order from ① to ⑤
① Begin at center. Ch 10, join with sl st to form ring.
  Row 1: Ch 3, dc 23 in ring.
  Row 2–12: Follow chart.
② Make braid, repeating ch 5, dc 5. When working inside loop, connect with motif 1 by sl st. While working dc of last row, connect end with first chain of foundation row by pulling each stitch together once.
③,④ Following chart, make braids on both sides.
⑤ Fill both spaces with two motifs.

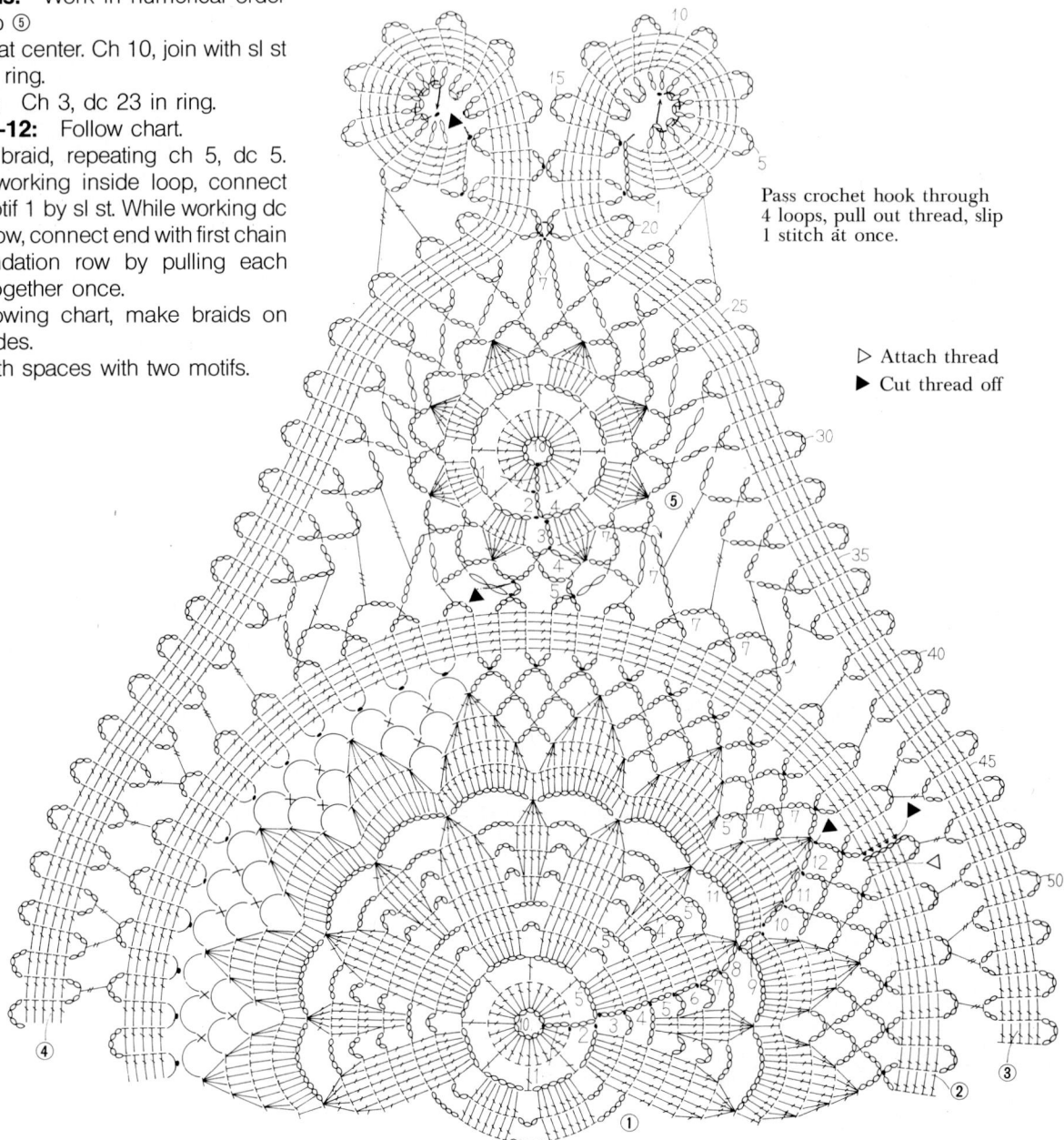

Pass crochet hook through 4 loops, pull out thread, slip 1 stitch at once.

▷ Attach thread
► Cut thread off

*Begin, making ring with ch 10.

4 Irish Doily

Materials: Anchor Mercer-Crochet no. ____ 30 white, 20 g
Steel crochet hook no. 8 (size 0.9 mm)

Finished Size: 28 cm (11″) in diameter

Directions: Work in numerical order from ① to ⑤.

① **Row 1:** Ch 10, dc 1 in 6th ch, dc 4 in each ch, turn.

Row 2: Ch 5, dc 5, turn.

Row 3–57: While repeating row 2, make braid following chart; at same time, connect 6 motifs around.

② At center of ①, while making motif, connect ① following chart. Connect ends after row 24, following directions on page 92.

③ Make braid, following chart.

④ Make motifs for filling space, following chart.

⑤ Work edging, 2 rows all around.

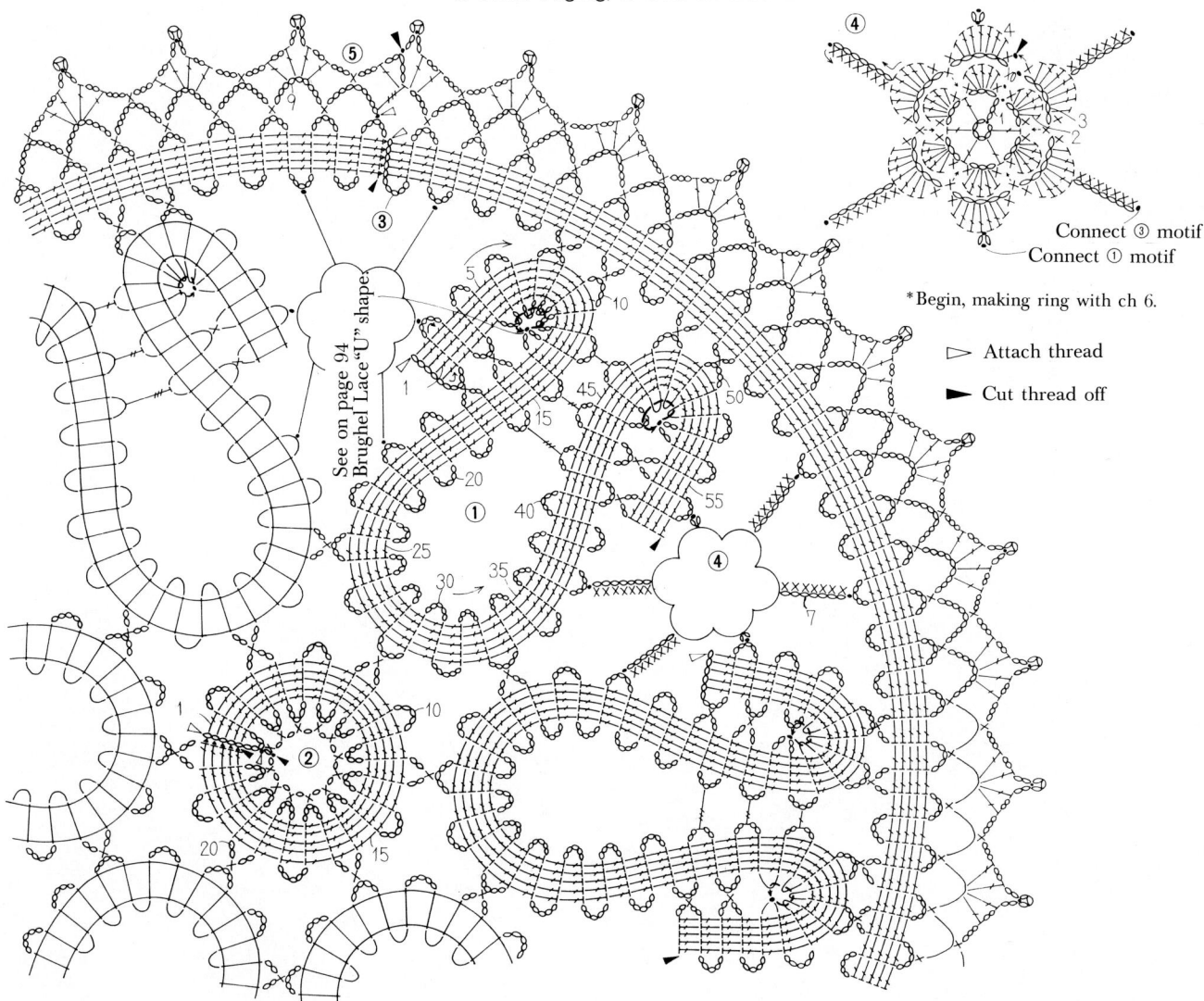

Connect ③ motif
Connect ① motif

*Begin, making ring with ch 6.

▷ Attach thread

► Cut thread off

See on page 94
Brughel Lace"U" shape

11

5

5 Margaret Doily

Materials: Anchor Mercer-Crochet no. 10 white, 20 g
Steel crochet hook no. 6 (size 1.25 mm)
Finished Size: 25 cm (10") in diameter
Directions: Begin at center. Make loop at the end of thread.
Row 1: Ch 1, "sc 1, ch 20" 12 times in loop and cut thread off.
Row 2–17: Attach thread on one chain loop, work following chart. Work popcorn of last row at center stitch loop of chain.

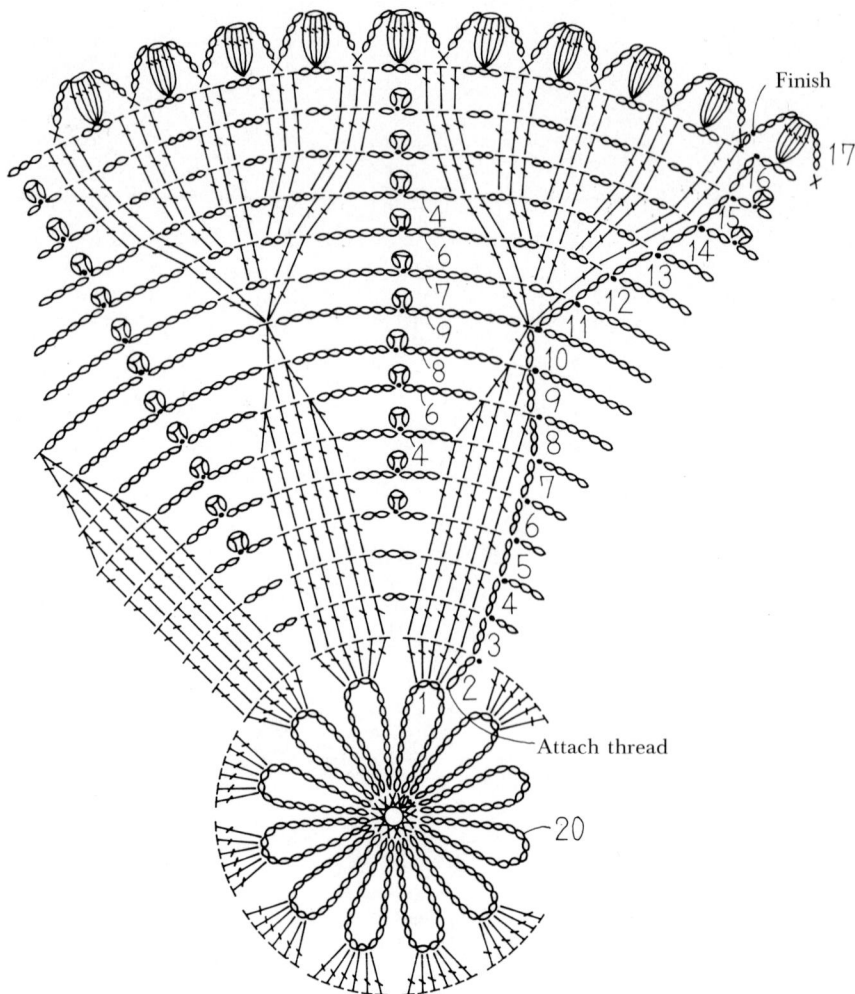

Finish

17
16
15
14
13
12
11
10
9
8
7
6
5
4
3
2
1

Attach thread

20

*Make loop at the end of thread.

6 Star Doily

Materials: Anchor Mercer-Crochet no. 30 white, 20 g
Steel crochet hook no. 8 (size 0.9 mm)
Finished Size: 25 cm (10″) in diameter
Directions: Ch 10, join with sl st to form ring.
Row 1: Ch 3, dc 23 in ring.
Row 2–22: Follow chart.

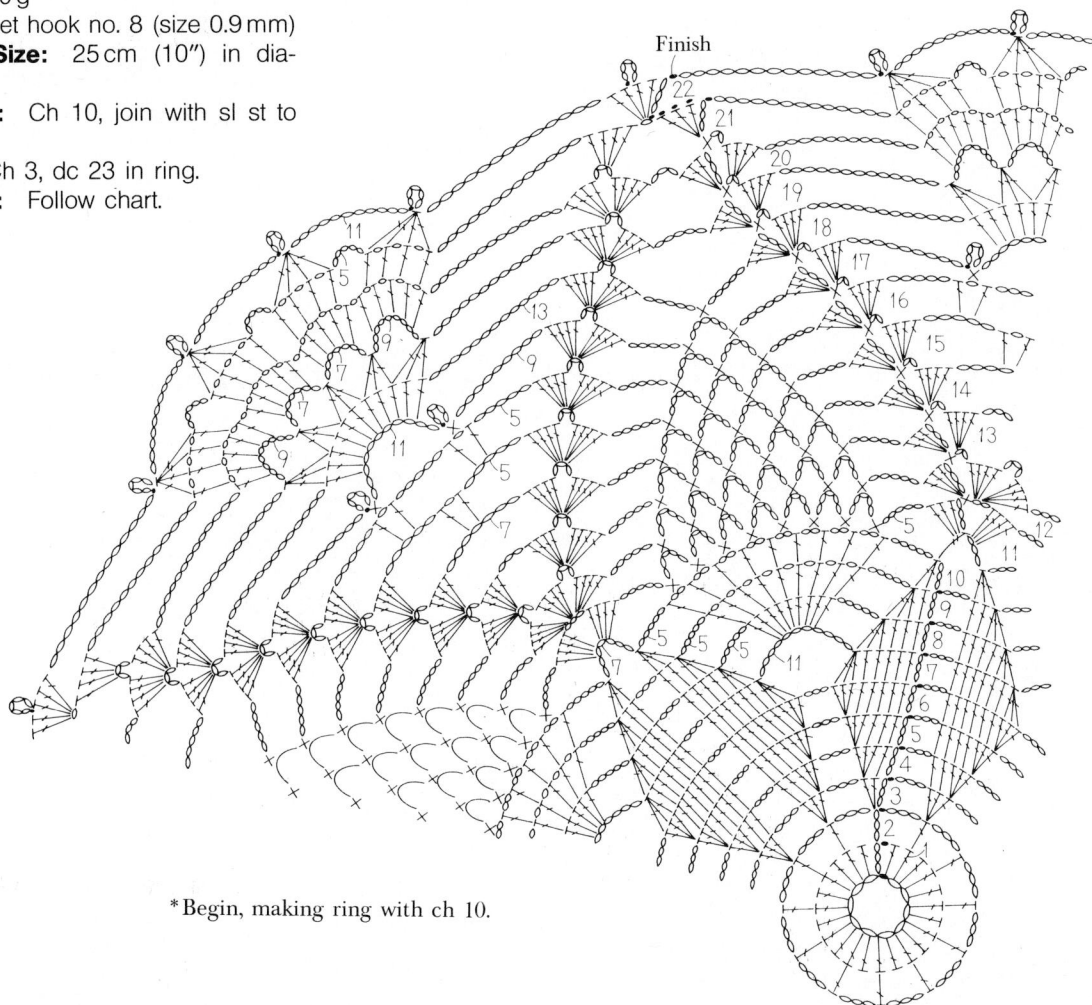

*Begin, making ring with ch 10.

Finish

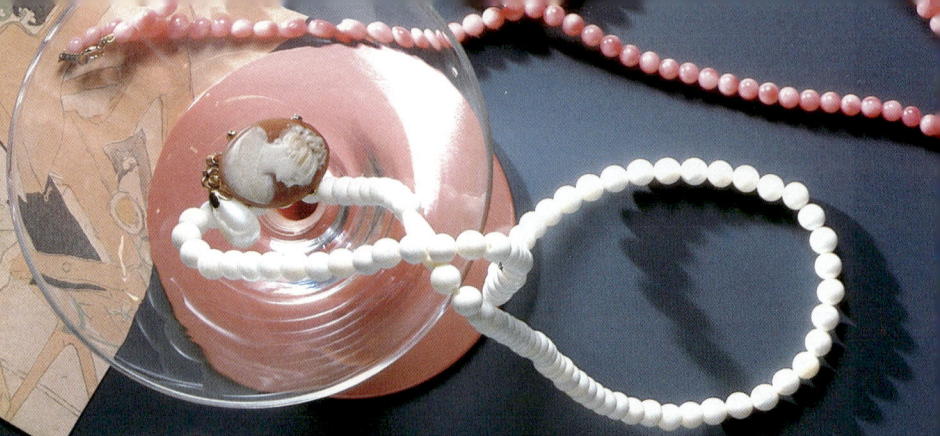

7
8
9

9 Doily

Materials: Anchor Mercer-Crochet no. 30 white, 20 g
Steel crochet hook no. 8 (size 0.9 mm)
Gauge: 10 cm (4") = 20 space, 19 rows
Finished Size: 15 × 28 cm (6 × 11")
Directions: Ch 91, work 54 rows in filet mesh, following chart.
Be careful to keep work flat.

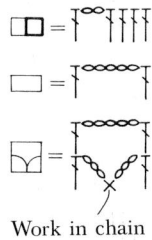

Work in chain

Filet Mesh Pattern Chart

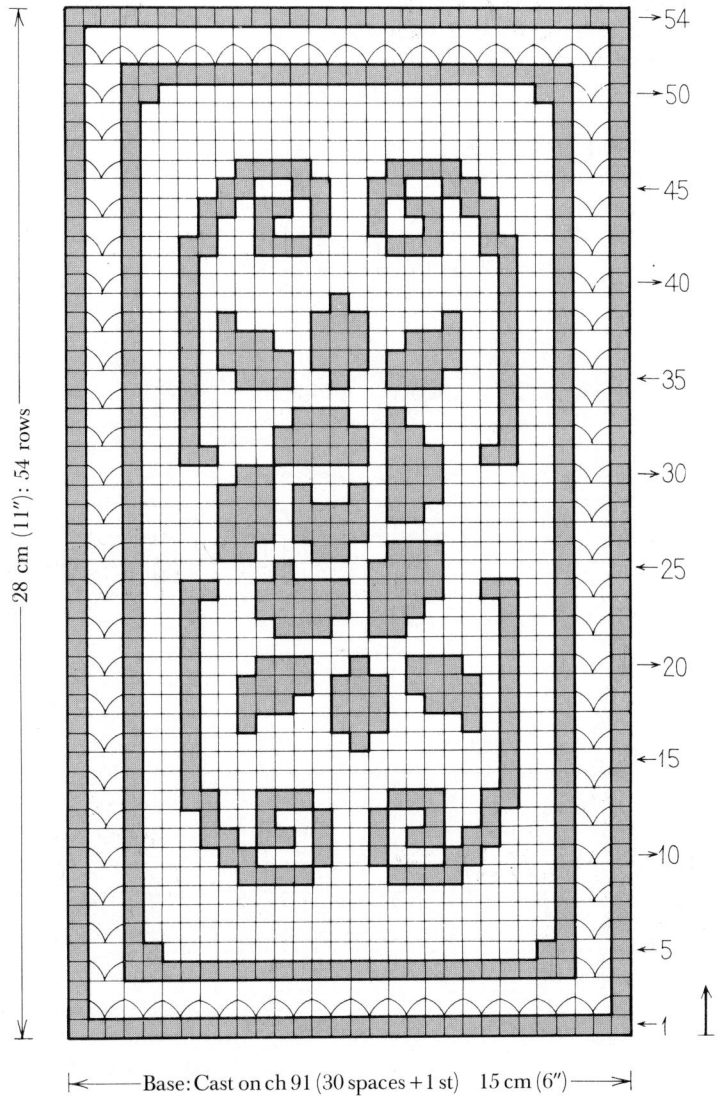

28 cm (11"): 54 rows

Base: Cast on ch 91 (30 spaces + 1 st)   15 cm (6")

8 Doily

Materials: Anchor Mercer-Crochet no. 30 white, 20 g
Steel crochet hook no. 8 (size 0.9 mm)
Finished Size: 20.5 cm (8″) square
Directions: Ch 6, join with sl st to form ring.
Row 1–19: Following chart, while increasing at four corners, work in filet mesh pattern.
Row 20: While working sc, following chart, work picots of 3-ch, 5-ch, and 3-ch.

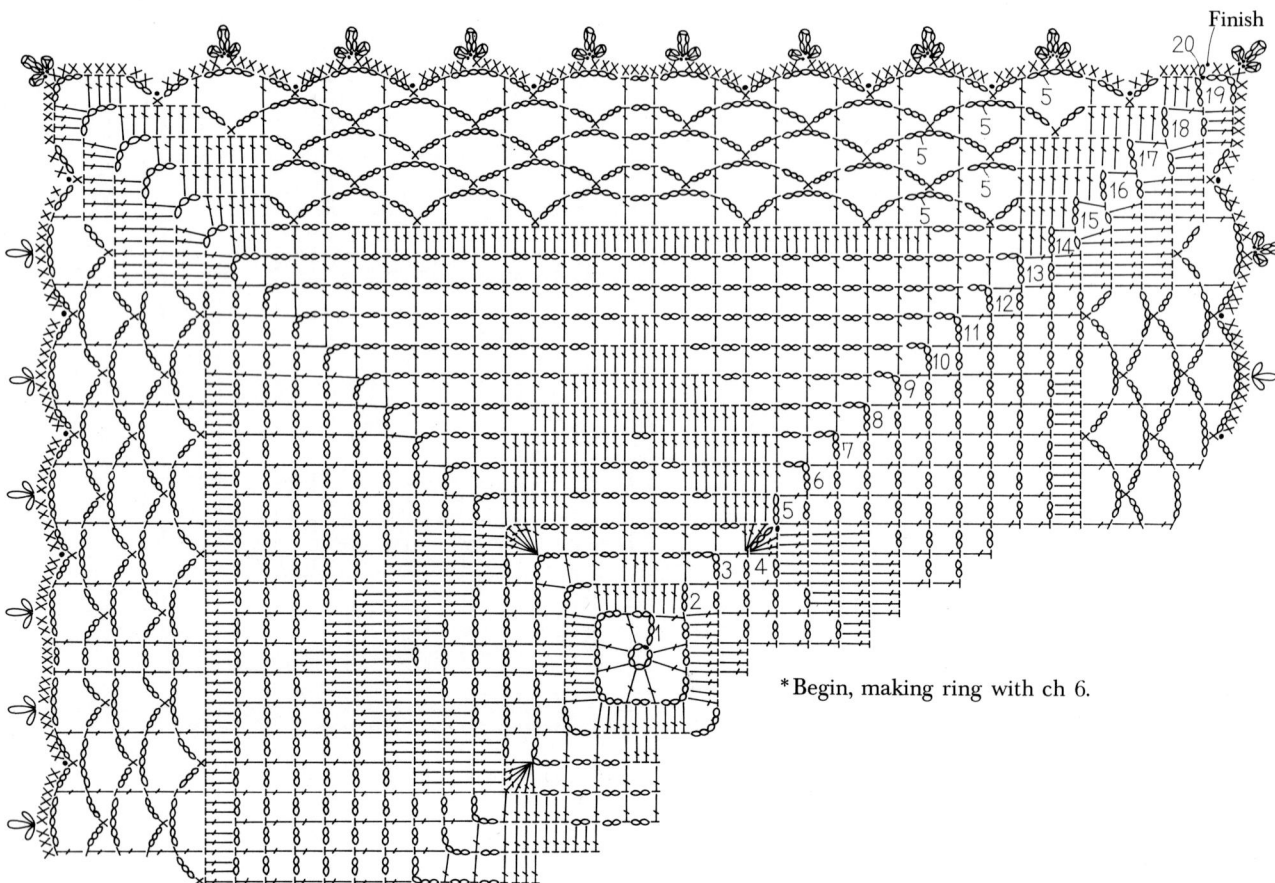

Finish

* Begin, making ring with ch 6.

7 Doily

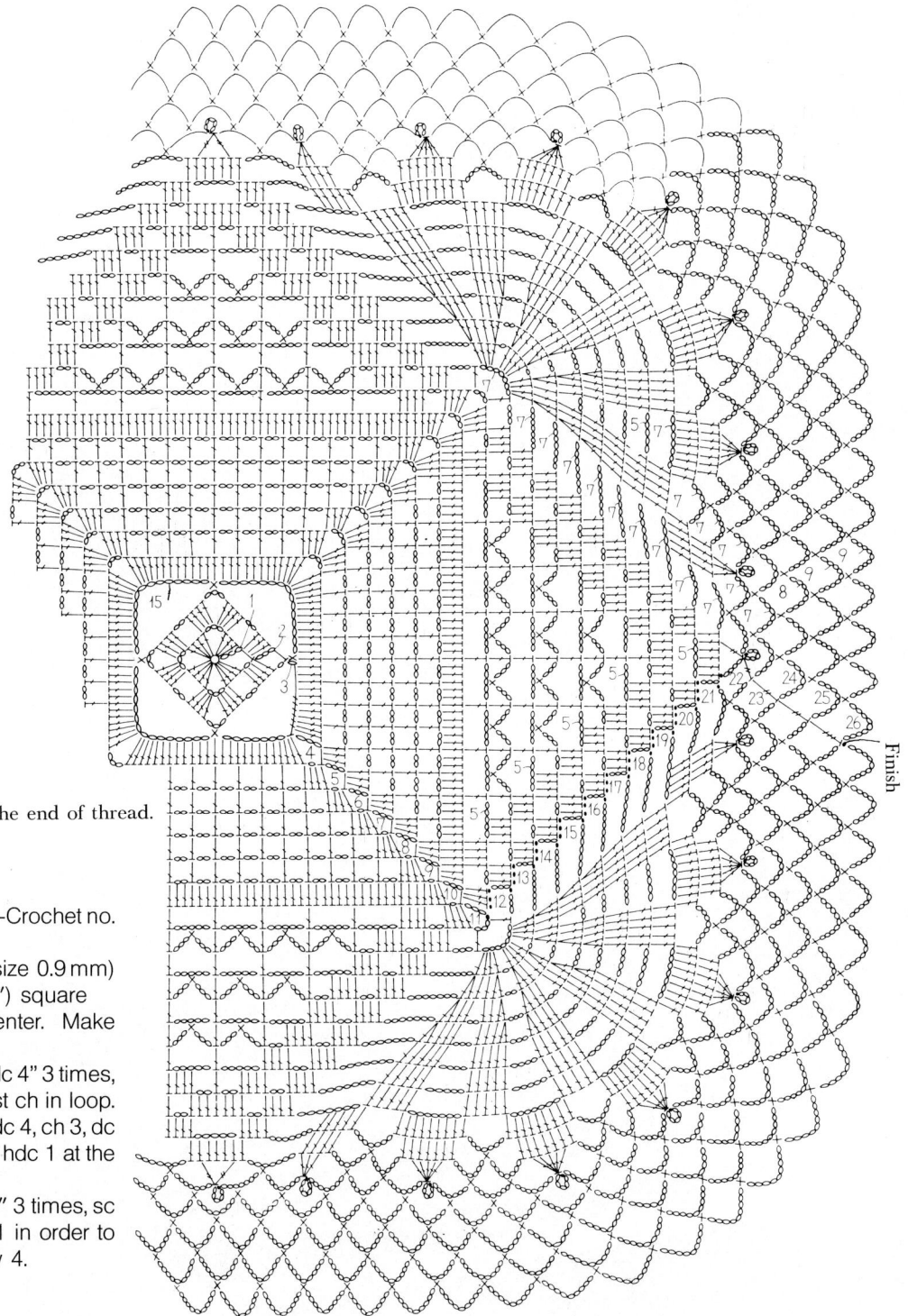

*Make loop at the end of thread.

Materials: Anchor Mercer-Crochet no. 30 white, 20 g
Steel crochet hook no. 8 (size 0.9 mm)
Finished Size: 21 cm (8″) square
Directions: Begin at center. Make loop at the end of thread.
Row 1: Ch 3, dc 3, "ch 3, dc 4" 3 times, ch 1, hdc 1 at the top of first ch in loop.
Row 2: Ch 3, dc 3, "ch 2, dc 4, ch 3, dc 4" 3 times, ch 2, dc 4, ch 1, hdc 1 at the top of first ch.
Row 3: Ch 1, "sc 1, ch 15" 3 times, sc 1, ch 7 six times; crochet 1 in order to begin at the corner for row 4.
Row 4–26: Follow chart.

18

Crochet for the Home
Arrangements for the Table, Cushions, Centerpieces, and Lace Pictures

10 ⃝ Table Set

Materials: Anchor Mercer-Crochet no. 40 light blue, 70 g for tablecloth; 10 g for tray mat; 20 g for cushion.
Steel crochet hook no. 8 (size 0.9 mm); light blue linen 92×110 cm (36×44″) for tablecloth; 37×27 cm (15×11″) for tray mat; 89×46 cm (36×18″) for cushion; 30 cm (12″) zipper; inner cushion filled with kapok.
Finished Sizes: Tablecloth 117×99 cm (44¼×39⅝″); tray mat 38×28 cm (15¼×11¼″); cushion 43 cm (17″) square.

Directions: See table set, p. 40; work around fabric and motif A in same manner.
Tablecloth: Finish 4 pieces of cloth with sc. Beginning at center motif, make and connect designs to cloth, following chart.
Tray Mat: Following chart, cut circle out of cloth as indicated, adding 3 mm (⅛″) seam allowance; turn in right side. Place motif A on right side and baste on wrong side. Sew around motif on right side.

Cushion: Cut cloth to size indicated, adding 1.5 cm (⅝″) seam allowance. Make opening at center back, attach zipper and machine stitch around it. Make and join motif A and appliqué at place indicated, following chart.

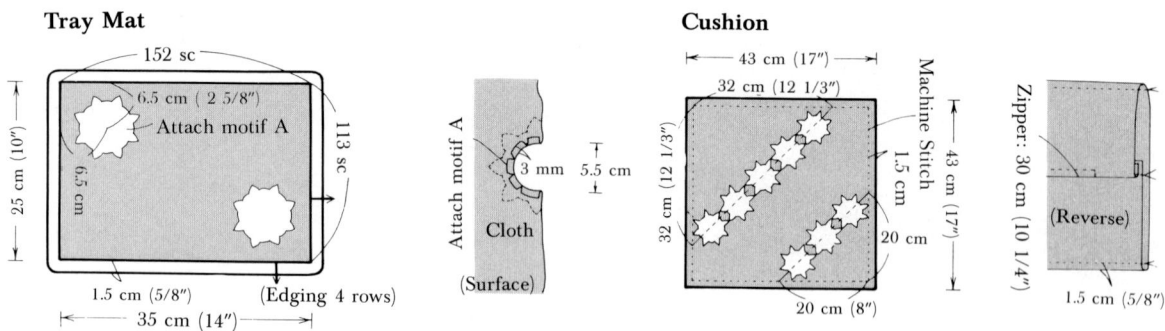

Tray Mat

152 sc
6.5 cm (2 5/8″)
Attach motif A
6.5 cm
25 cm (10″)
113 sc
1.5 cm (5/8″)
(Edging 4 rows)
35 cm (14″)

Motif A same as
　　Motif A of page 40.

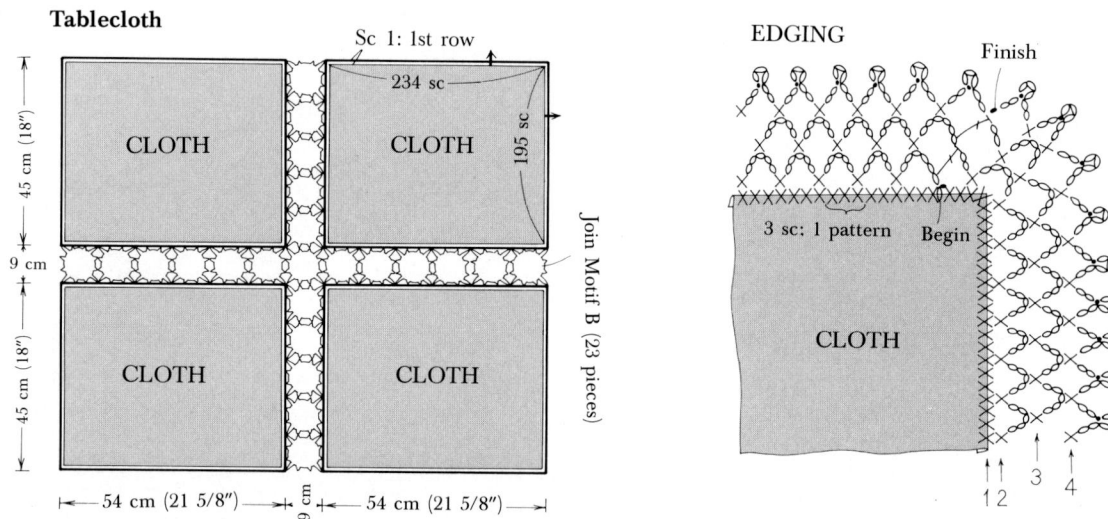

Attach motif A
3 mm
5.5 cm
Cloth
(Surface)

Cushion

43 cm (17″)
32 cm (12 1/3″)
Machine Stitch
32 cm (12 1/3″)
1.5 cm
43 cm (17″)
20 cm
20 cm (8″)

Zipper: 30 cm (10 1/4″)
(Reverse)
1.5 cm (5/8″)

Tablecloth

Sc 1: 1st row
234 sc
195 sc
CLOTH
CLOTH
CLOTH
CLOTH
45 cm (18″)
9 cm
45 cm (18″)
Join Motif B (23 pieces)
54 cm (21 5/8″)
9 cm
54 cm (21 5/8″)

EDGING

Finish
3 sc: 1 pattern
Begin
CLOTH
1 2 3 4

24

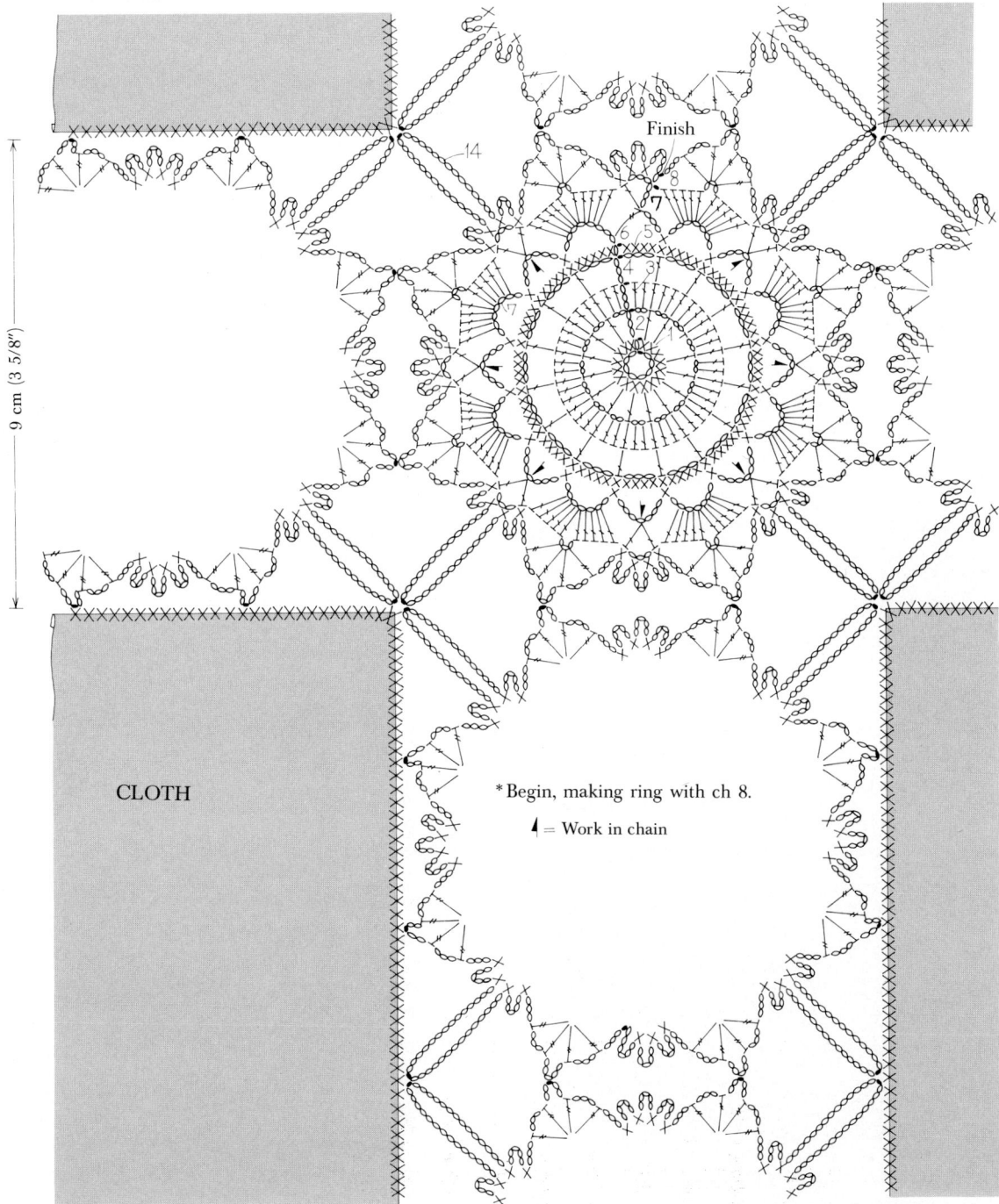

MOTIF B

9 cm (3 5/8")

14

Finish

8

7

6 5

4 3

1

2

CLOTH

*Begin, making ring with ch 8.

= Work in chain

25

11 Romantic Cushion A

Materials: Anchor Mercer-Crochet no. 30 white, 10 g
Steel crochet hook no. 8 (size 0.9 mm); white lawn 1 m (39") × 90 cm (36") wide; white tulle 15 cm (6") square; embroidered 1.5 cm (⅝") tape, 70 cm (28") length. Inner cushion filled with kapok.

Finished Size: 35 cm (14") square

Directions: Cut lawn, adding 1 cm (½") seam allowance; use both selvages for ruffle.

Center tulle on front of cushion; attach embroidered tape around it with tiny slip stitches.

Make flowers and 8 crocheted cords (see page 98).

Attach them to the tulle, following design, with tiny slip stitches.

With right sides of front and back together, and the ruffle in between, stitch all around, leaving 17 cm (7") of back open. Insert cushion and sew up opening.

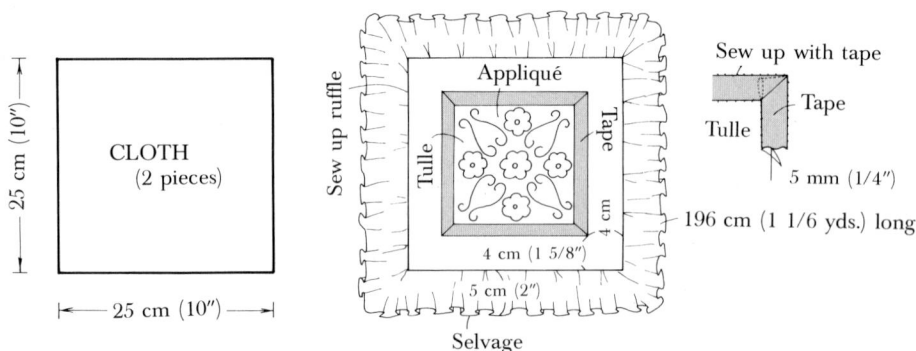

CLOTH
(2 pieces)

25 cm (10")

25 cm (10")

Sew up ruffle

Appliqué

Tulle

Tape

4 cm

4 cm (1 5/8")

5 cm (2")

Selvage

Sew up with tape

Tape

Tulle

5 mm (1/4")

196 cm (1 1/6 yds.) long

Appliqué Pattern Chart

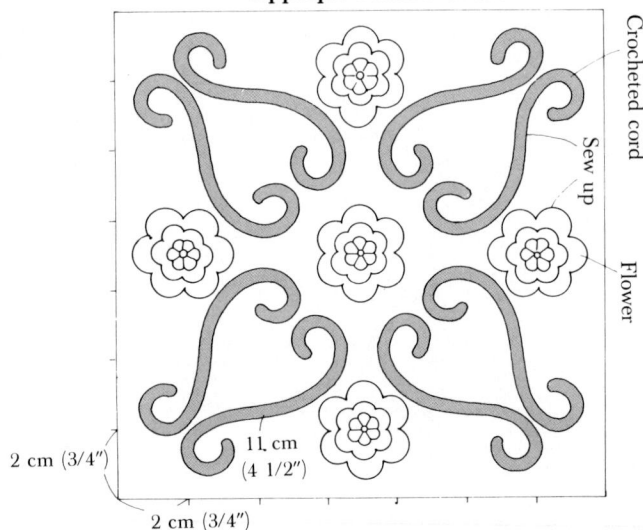

Crocheted cord

Sew up

Flower

2 cm (3/4")

11 cm (4 1/2")

2 cm (3/4")

FLOWER (5 pieces)

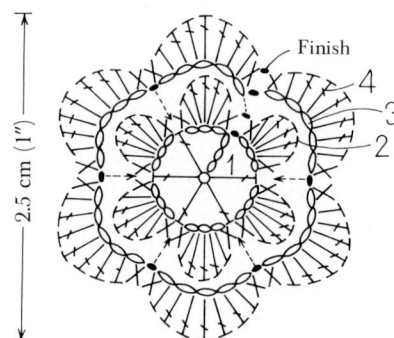

Finish

4
3
2
1

2.5 cm (1")

*Make loop at the end of thread.

12 Romantic Cushion B

Materials: Anchor Mercer-Crochet no. 30 white, 10 g; pink, 5 g.
Steel crochet hook no. 8 (size 0.9 mm); white lawn 82 cm (32⅛") long × 90 cm (36"); 1.2 cm (½")-wide embroidered tape, 50 cm (20") length. Inner cushion filled with kapok.

Finished Size: 36 cm (14½") in diameter

Directions: Follow directions for A to make cushion.

Work A and B ruffles and center flower. Attach ruffles on front of cushion.

Insert inner cushion. Attach flower to center front, sewing through to the back with pink crochet cotton no. 30.

FLOWER (Pink)

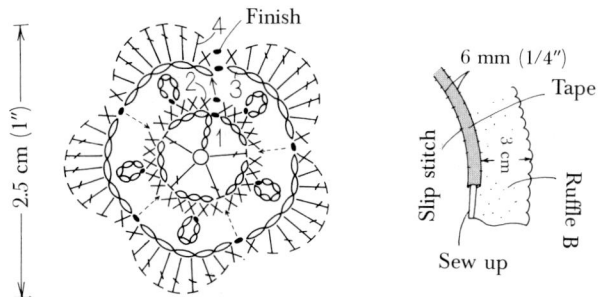

*Make loop at the end of thread.

CLOTH (2 pieces)

Tape

15 cm (6")

26 cm (10 1/2")

Ruffle B

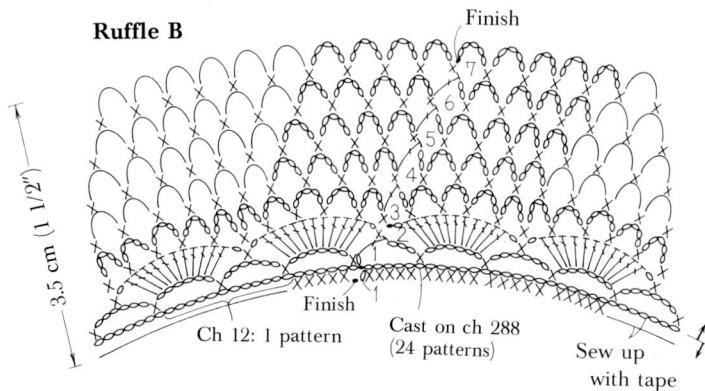

Ch 12: 1 pattern

Cast on ch 288 (24 patterns)

Sew up with tape

Finish

3.5 cm (1 1/2")

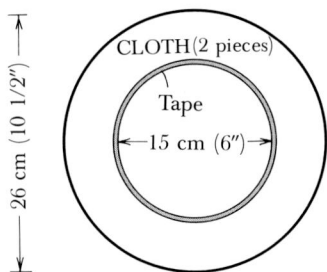

Selvage

5 cm (2")

Sew up ruffle B

Ruffle B

Tape

Ruffle A

Flower

Sew up ruffle A

Sew up ruffle 160 cm (1 1/4 yds.) long

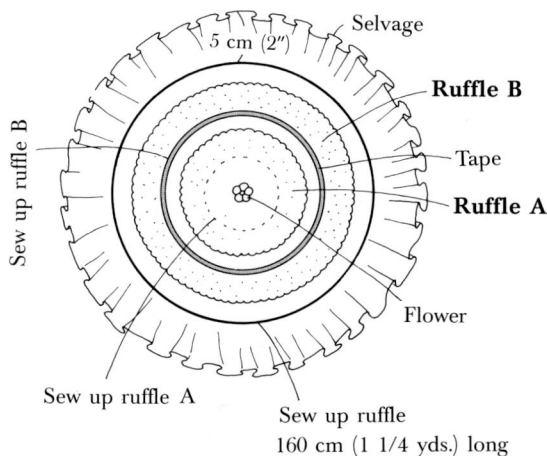

Ruffle A

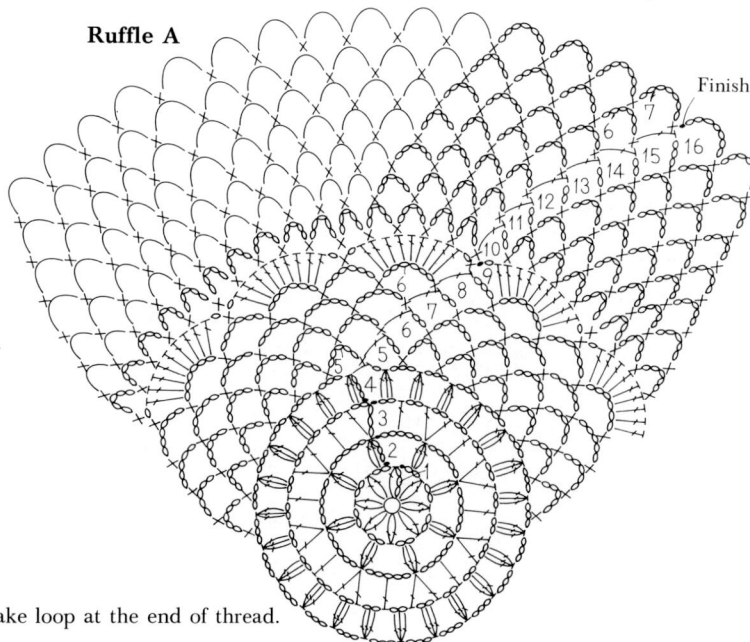

Finish

*Make loop at the end of thread.

Materials: Anchor Mercer-Crochet no. 30 white, 10 g; lavender, 5 g
Steel crochet hook #8 (size 0.9 mm); white lawn 82 cm (32⅞″) long × 90 cm (36″); white tulle 14 cm (5½″) square; lavender satin ribbon 0.6 cm (¼″) wide, 1 m (39″) length. Inner cushion filled with kapok.
Finished Size: 35 × 36.5 cm (14 × 14⅝″)

Directions: Follow directions for A to make cushion.
Work large flower, small flowers, leaves, and 2 crocheted cords, following chart, and appliqué on front. Attach ribbon all around with tiny slip stitches and tie ends of ribbon.

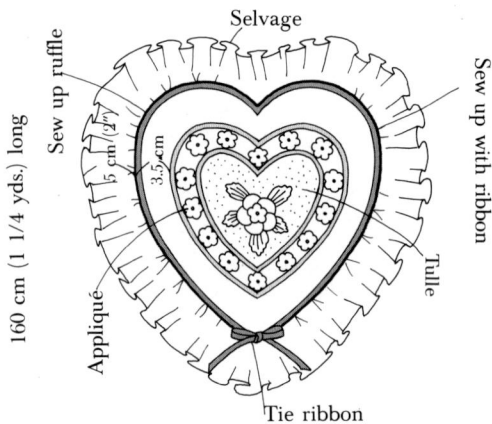

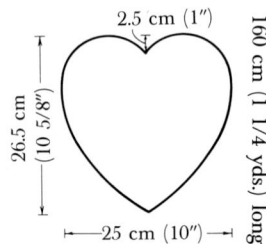

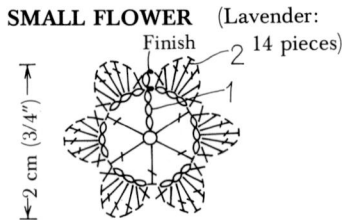

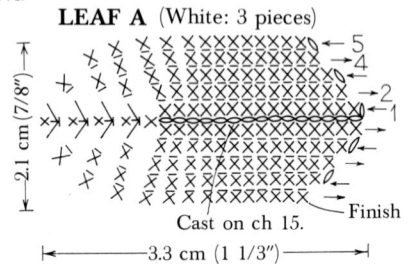

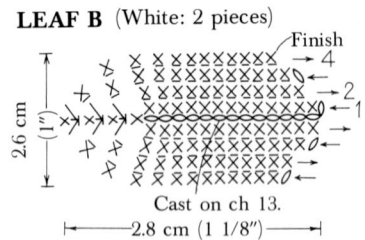

LEAF A (White: 3 pieces)
2.1 cm (7/8″)
Cast on ch 15.
3.3 cm (1 1/3″)
Finish

LEAF B (White: 2 pieces)
Finish
2.6 cm (1″)
Cast on ch 13.
2.8 cm (1 1/8″)

2.5 cm (1″)
26.5 cm (10 5/8″)
160 cm (1 1/4 yds.) long
25 cm (10″)

SMALL FLOWER (Lavender: 14 pieces)
Finish
2 cm (3/4″)

Selvage
Sew up ruffle
160 cm (1 1/4 yds.) long
5 cm (2″)
3.5 cm
Appliqué
Sew up with ribbon
Tulle
Tie ribbon

FLOWER (White: 1 piece)
Slip the reverse of the last row.
5 cm (2″)

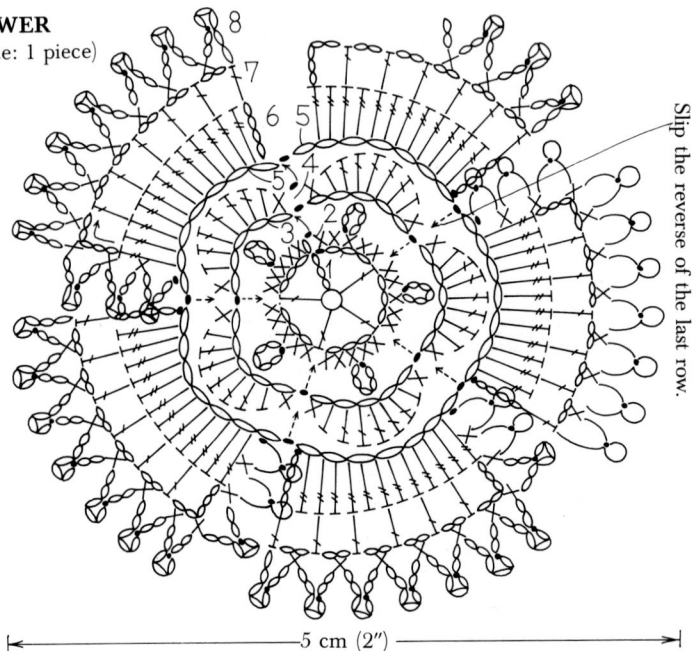

Appliqué Pattern Chart

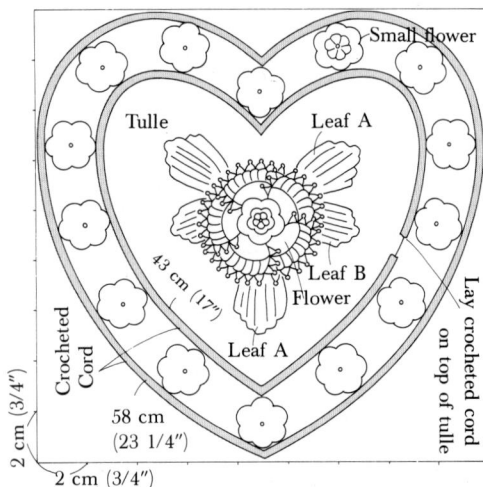

Small flower
Tulle
Leaf A
Leaf B
Flower
Leaf A
Crocheted Cord
43 cm (17″)
58 cm (23 1/4″)
Lay crocheted cord on top of tulle
2 cm (3/4″)
2 cm (3/4″)

*Make loop at the end of thread.

14 Cushion

Materials: Anchor Mercer-Crochet no. 30 white, 50 g for A and 40 g, for B. Steel crochet hook no. 8 (size 0.9 mm); 2 ready-made pillows, 41 cm (16") square.

Gauge: 10 cm (4") = 20 spaces and 20 rows

Finished Size: A = 30 cm (12") square; B = 27 cm (11") square

Directions: Work both in filet mesh, following chart. Work 2 rows of edging.

Following photograph, attach mesh designs to each pillow with tiny slip stitches.

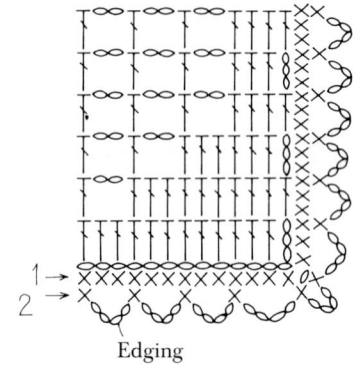

1 →
2 →

Edging

Mesh Pattern Chart

50

45

40

35

30

25

20

15

10

5

1st row

26 cm (10 1/2"): 52 rows

← 26 cm (10 1/2") Base: Cast on ch 157 (52 sps +1 st) →

15 Cushion

Mesh Pattern Chart

29 cm (10 1/8"): 58 rows

55
50
45
40
35
30
25
20
15
10
5
1st row

← 29 cm (10 1/8") Base: Cast on ch 175 (58 sps +1 st) →

16 Lace Picture

Materials: Anchor Mercer-Crochet no. 30 white, 10 g
Steel crochet hook no. 8 (0.9 mm); light green linen 21 cm × 27 cm (8¼ × 11⅝″); square frame, inside measurement 14 × 19.5 cm (6½ × 8″); 1 white pearl bead, 2 round blue beads, 9 round beads in the color of your choice.

Finished Size: See diagram
Directions: Make necessary number of flowers and leaves.
Work crocheted cord and sl st chain cord for tree and branch, following chart.
Work crocheted cord for birds and man.
Trace design onto cloth and attach each motif with tiny slip stitches.

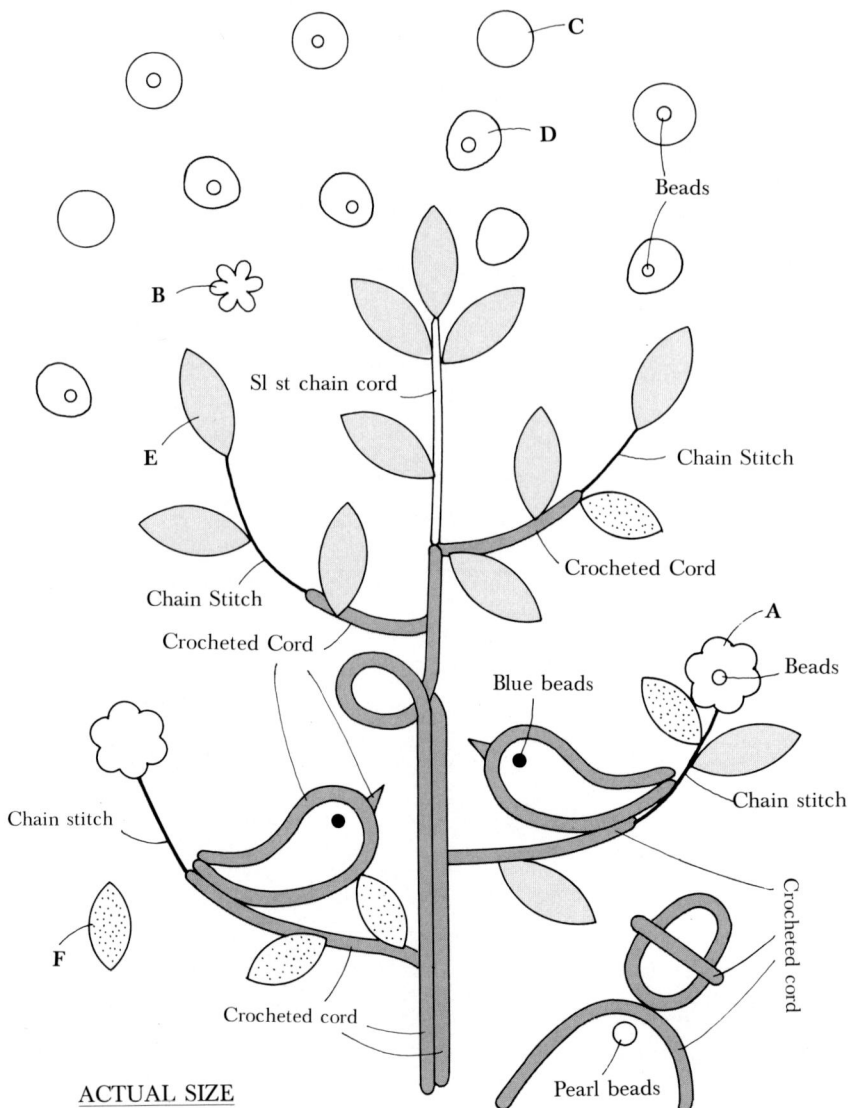

C

D

Beads

B

Sl st chain cord

Chain Stitch

E

Chain Stitch

Crocheted Cord

Crocheted Cord

Blue beads

A

Beads

Chain stitch

Chain stitch

F

Crocheted cord

Crocheted cord

Pearl beads

ACTUAL SIZE

FLOWER

A (2 pieces)   **B** (1 piece)

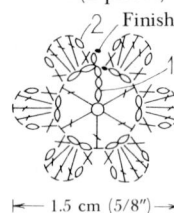   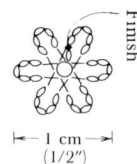

Finish   Finish

|← 1.5 cm (5/8″) →| |← 1 cm (1/2″) →|

*Make loop at the end of thread.

C (5 pieces)   **D** (6 pieces)

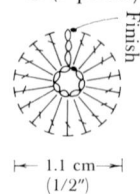   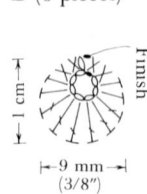

Finish   Finish

|← 1.1 cm (1/2″) →| |← 9 mm (3/8″) →|

*Begin, making ring with ch 7.

LEAF

E (12 pieces)

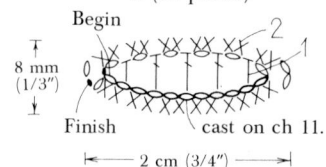

Begin   2   1
8 mm (1/3″)
Finish   cast on ch 11.

|← 2 cm (3/4″) →|

F (5 pieces)

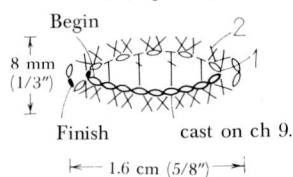

Begin   2   1
8 mm (1/3″)
Finish   cast on ch 9.

|← 1.6 cm (5/8″) →|

Sl st chain cord

Begin ◦-●-◦-●-◦-●-◦-●-◦

17 Lace Picture

Materials: Anchor Mercer-Crochet no. 30 white, 15 g
Steel crochet hook no. 8 (size 0.9 mm); lavender fabric 18×23 cm (7×9″); square frame, inner measurement 11×15.5 cm (4½×6″).
Size: 11×15.5 cm (4½×6″).
Directions: Trace design on fabric. Make necessary number of flowers and leaves, following chart. Crochet cord (see p. 93)—75 cm (30″) length for the border and outline of girl.

Sew cord onto design on fabric with tiny slip stitches and cut off unused cord.

For pleats of skirt, make chain of crocheted cord and attach each pleat separately with tiny slip stitches.

For scarf, work on crocheted cord, fold back, and attach with tiny stitches.

Attach flowers and leaves with tiny slip stitches.

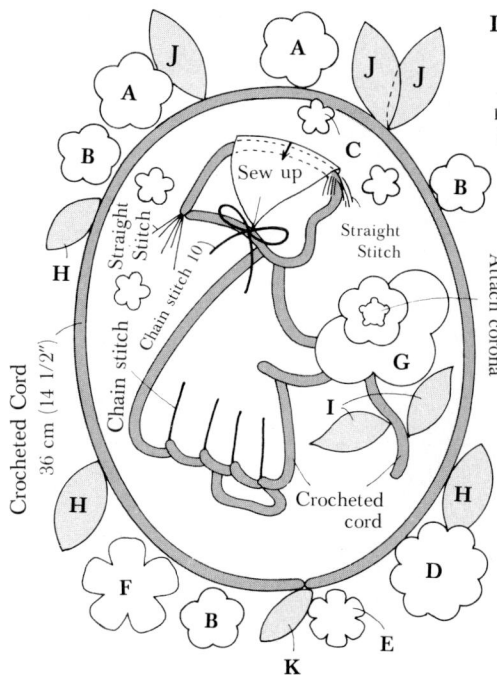

LEAF

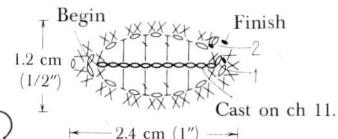

H (3 pieces)

Begin · Finish
1.2 cm (1/2″) · Cast on ch 11.
2.4 cm (1″)

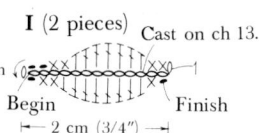

I (2 pieces) · Cast on ch 13.
9 mm · Begin · Finish
2 cm (3/4″)

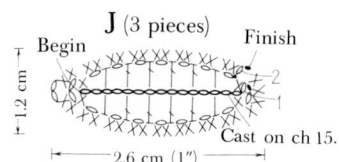

J (3 pieces)
Begin · Finish
1.2 cm
Cast on ch 15.
2.6 cm (1″)

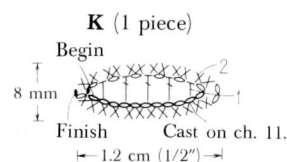

K (1 piece)
Begin
8 mm · Finish · Cast on ch. 11.
1.2 cm (1/2″)

FLOWER

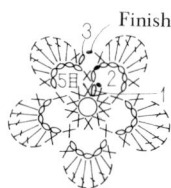

A (2 pieces)
Finish
2 cm (3/4″)

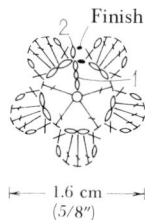

B (3 pieces)
Finish
1.6 cm (5/8″)

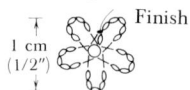

C (4 pieces)
Finish
1 cm (1/2″)

E (1 piece)
Finish
1.4 cm (9/16″)

*Make loop at the end of thread.

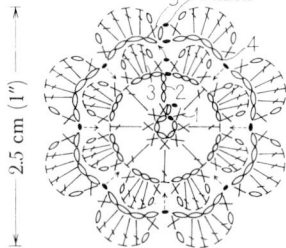

D (1 piece)
Finish
2.5 cm (1″)

*Begin, making ring with ch 5.

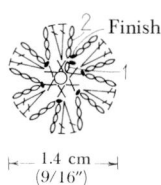

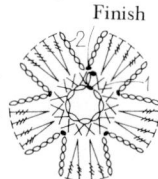

F (1 piece)
Finish
2.3 cm (7/8″)

*Begin, making ring with ch 8.

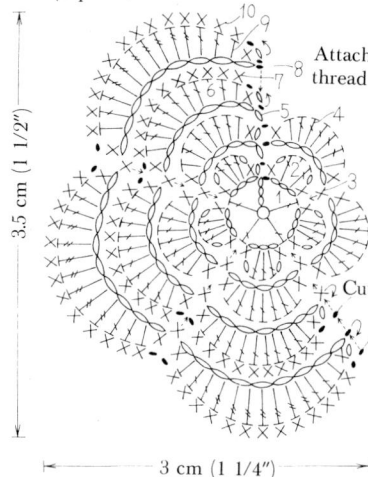

G (1 piece)
3.5 cm (1 1/2″)
Attach thread
Cut thread off
Finish
3 cm (1 1/4″)

*Make loop at the end of thread.

SCARF

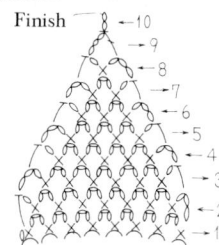

Finish

CORONA

(1 piece)

Finish

*Make loop at the end of thread.

37

18 Lovely Table Linens

Materials: Anchor Mercer-Crochet no. 40 (387), 60 g
Steel crochet hook no. 8 (size 0.9 mm); 2 pieces of ivory linen 35 cm (14″) square for napkin, 35 cm (14″) square for bread mat; 2 pieces 40 × 27 cm (16 × 11″) for luncheon mat.
Finished Size: Napkin and bread basket mats 35 cm (14″) square; luncheon mat 38 × 25 cm (15 × 10″).

Directions:
Bread Basket Mat: Cut out cloth along grain of fabric, following diagram, adding 3 mm (⅛″) seam allowance. Pull a thread 5 mm (¼″) in from edge and fold in half. Work sc around cloth, inserting hook into line of pulled threads; work 2 rows of edging. Make 4 motifs A and attach at four corners of cloth.

Napkin: Make same size as bread basket mat but attach only 1 motif.
Luncheon Mat: Cut out cloth, following diagram and adding hem allowance. Work edging in same manner as bread basket mat. Make and join motif B to two cut corners.

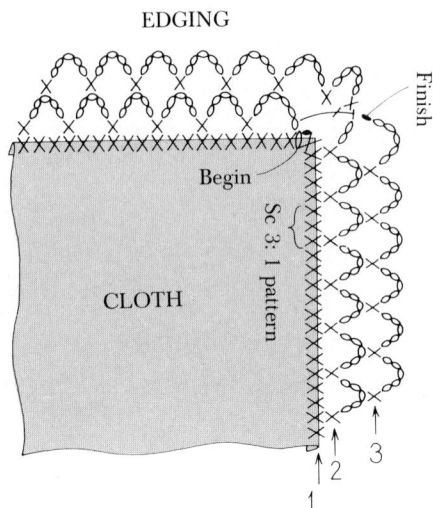

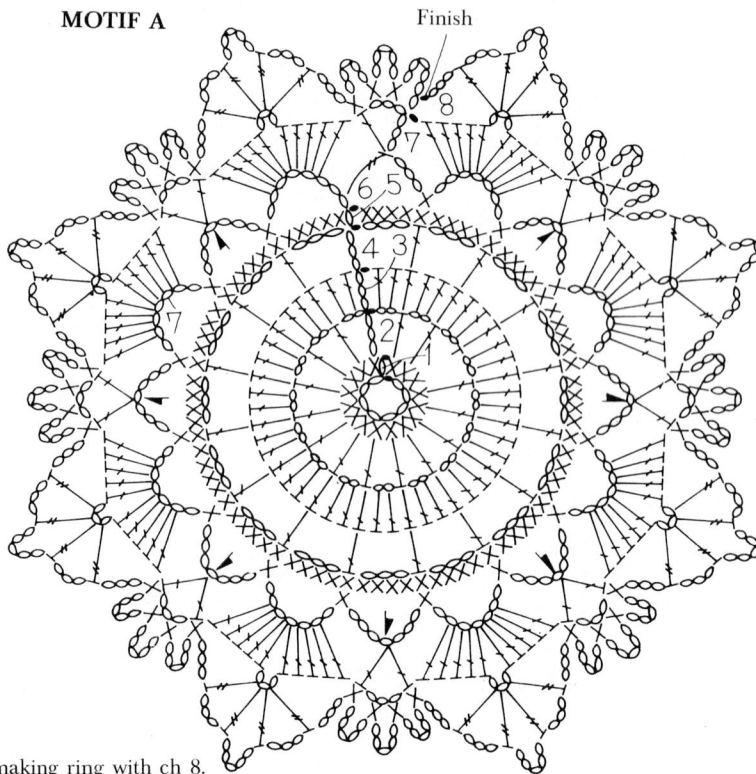

EDGING

MOTIF A

Finish

Begin

Sc 3: 1 pattern

CLOTH

1 2 3

*Begin, making ring with ch 8.

|← —— 9 cm (3 5/8″) —— →|

Bread Basket Mat

Work 3 rows of edging

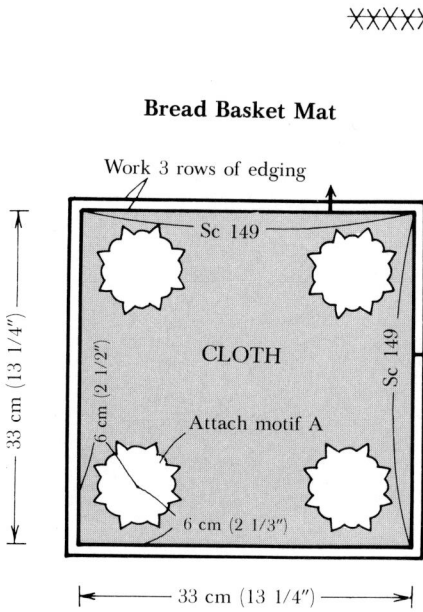

Sc 149

Sc 149

CLOTH

6 cm (2 1/2")

Attach motif A

6 cm (2 1/3")

33 cm (13 1/4")

33 cm (13 1/4")

Luncheon Mat

Work Sc 1 round of edging

MOTIF B

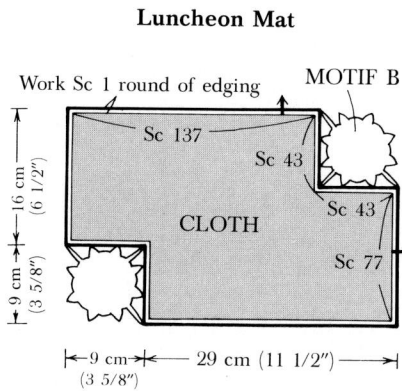

Sc 137

Sc 43

Sc 43

Sc 77

CLOTH

9 cm (3 5/8")

16 cm (6 1/2")

9 cm (3 5/8")

29 cm (11 1/2")

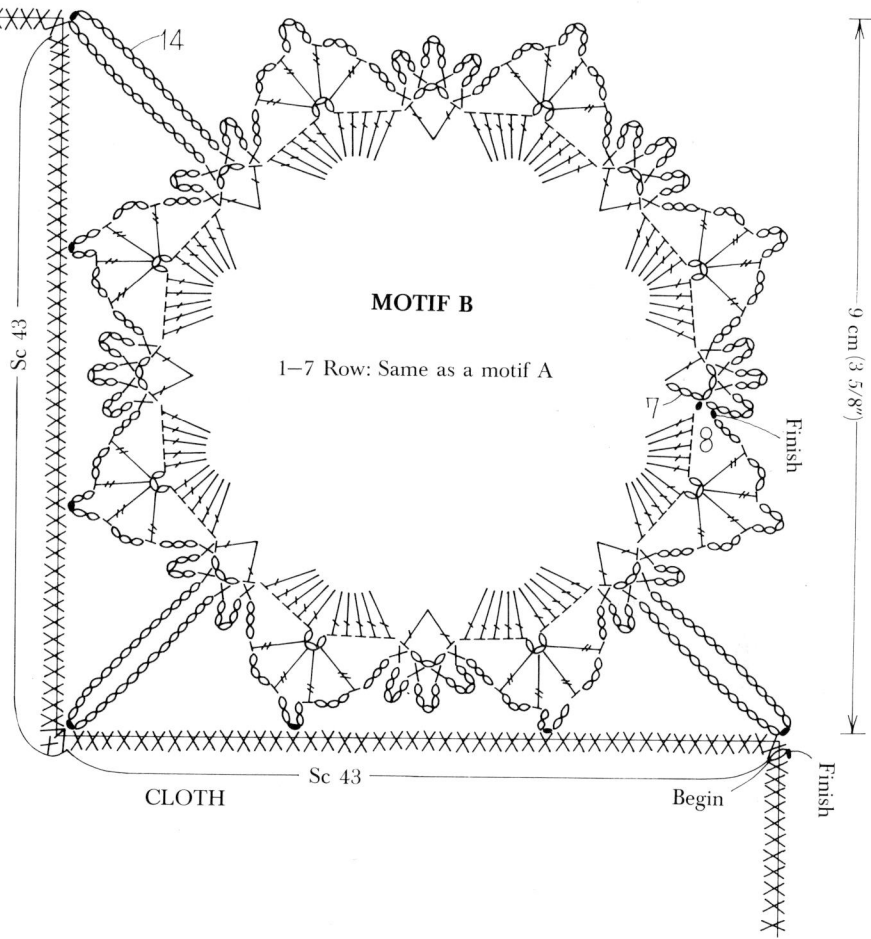

MOTIF B

1–7 Row: Same as a motif A

Sc 43

9 cm (3 5/8")

Finish

Finish

Begin

CLOTH

Sc 43

CLOTH

19 Table Center

Materials: Anchor Mercer-Crochet no. 30 (387), 40 g
Steel crochet hook no. 8 (size 0.9 mm); beige linen 61 cm × 26 cm (24 × 10½″)
Gauge: 1 motif = 8.5 cm (3⅜″) square
Finished Size: Approximately 62 × 35 cm (24½ × 14″)
Directions: Make 7 motifs, following chart. While working one motif, connect the next.

Cut linen in half lengthwise, along grain of fabric.

Pull thread 4 mm (⅛″) in from edge of cloth; fold that edge in half and work 1 row of sc all around.

Join motifs to linen with slip stitches. Work 1 row of edging.

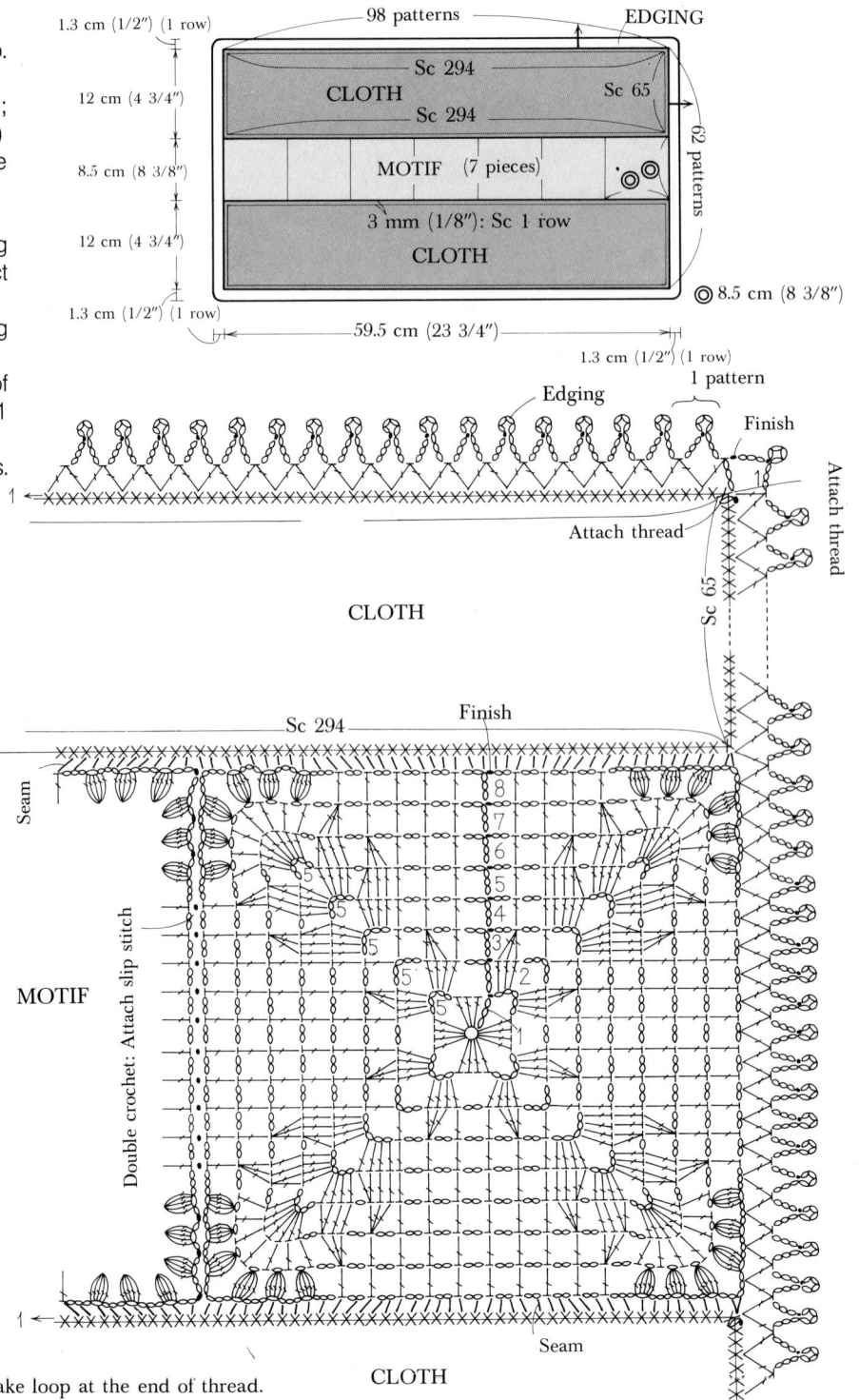

1.3 cm (1/2″) (1 row) 98 patterns EDGING

Sc 294
CLOTH   Sc 65
12 cm (4 3/4″)   Sc 294

8.5 cm (8 3/8″)   MOTIF (7 pieces)   62 patterns

3 mm (1/8″): Sc 1 row
12 cm (4 3/4″)   CLOTH

1.3 cm (1/2″) (1 row)   ◎ 8.5 cm (8 3/8″)

59.5 cm (23 3/4″)

1.3 cm (1/2″) (1 row)
1 pattern

Edging   Finish

Attach thread

Attach thread

CLOTH   Sc 65

Sc 294   Finish

Seam

MOTIF

Double crochet: Attach slip stitch

8
7
6
5
4
3
2
1

Seam

*Make loop at the end of thread.

CLOTH

20 Table Center

Materials: Anchor Mercer-Crochet no. 30 white, 60 g
Steel crochet hook #8 (size 0.9 mm)
Finished Size: 54 × 43 cm (21 × 17")
Directions: Make 4 motifs. Ch 10, join with sl st to form ring. Work, following chart.

While working last row of second motif, connect to next motif. Work 16 rows of edging, following chart.

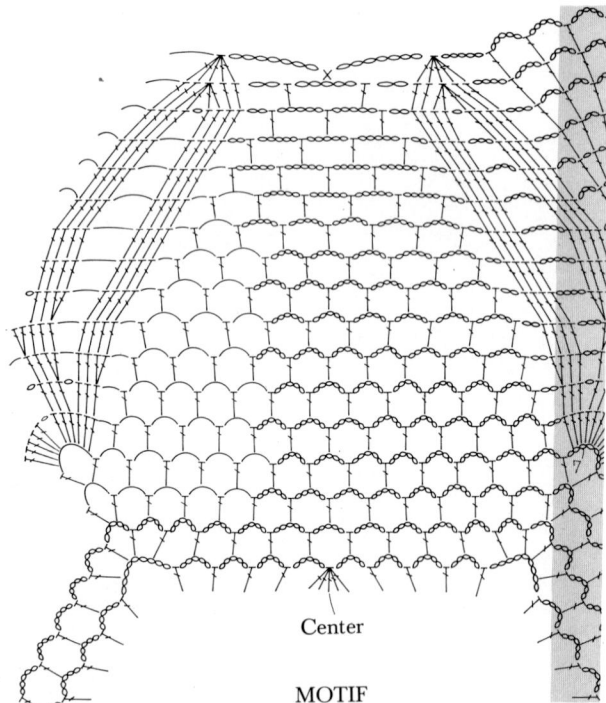

Chart for Joining

Finish

Center

MOTIF

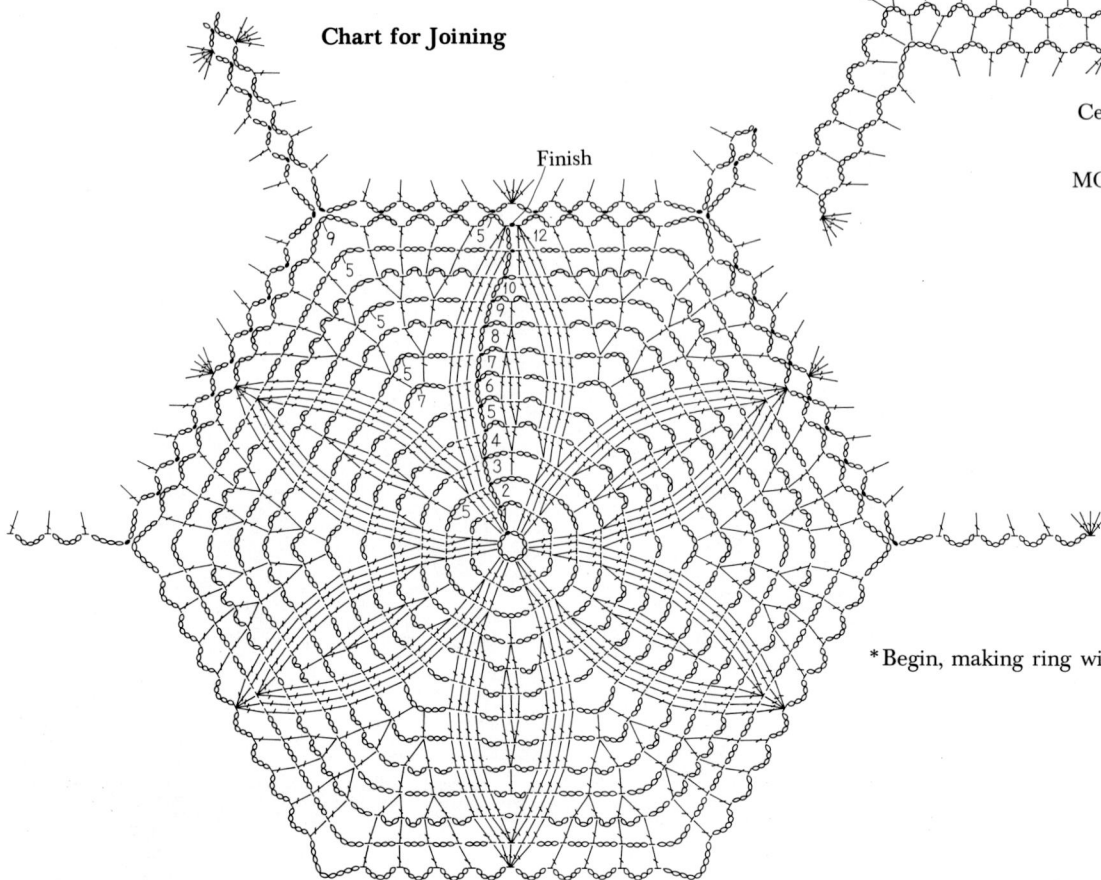

*Begin, making ring with ch 10.

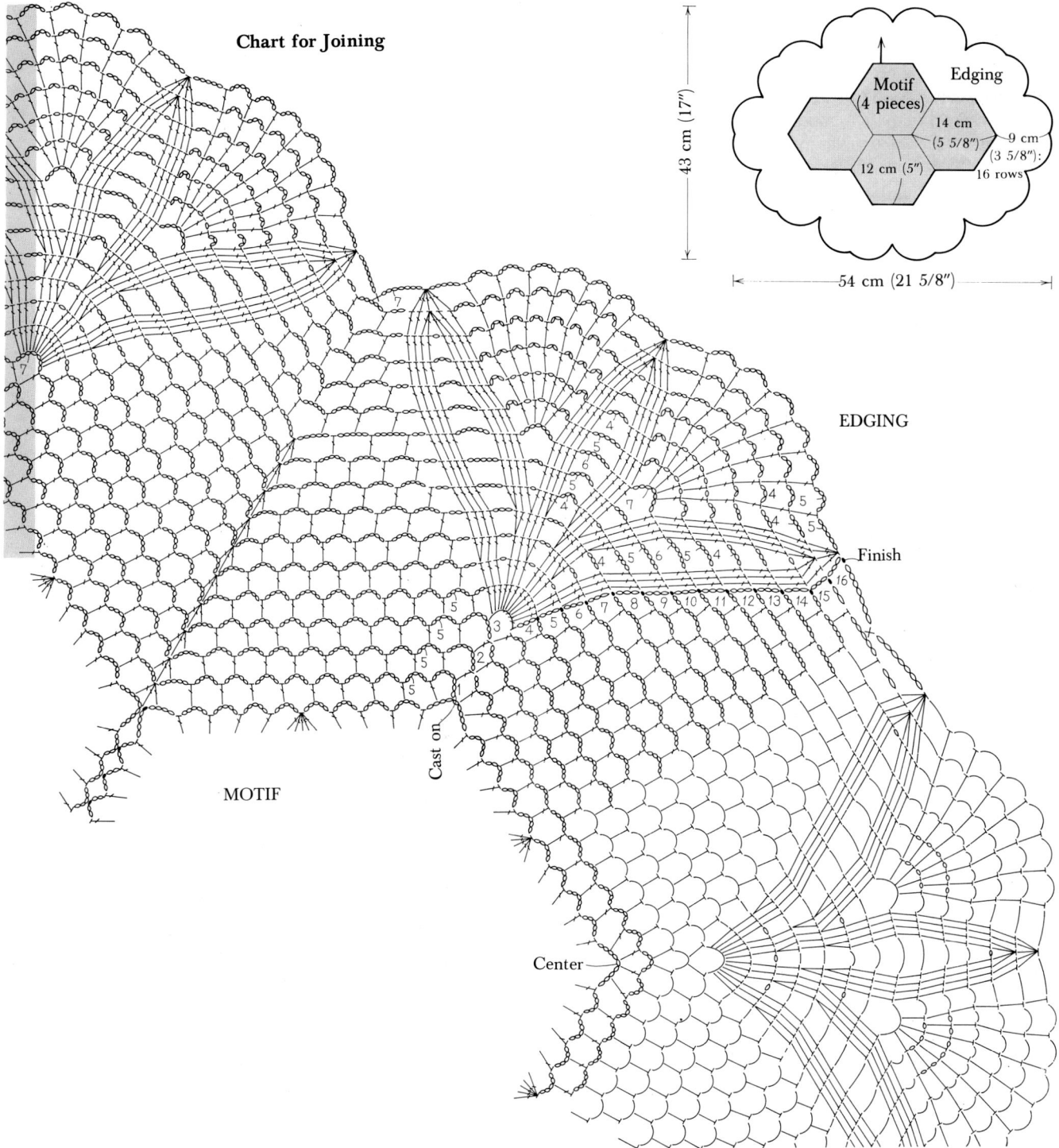

Chart for Joining

MOTIF

Cast on

Center

EDGING

Finish

Edging

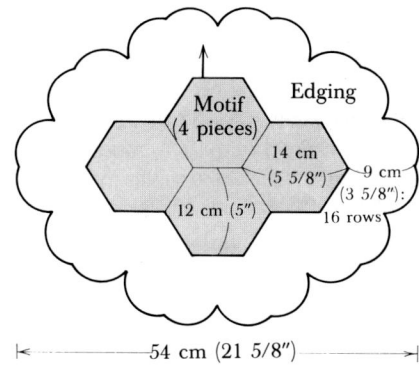

Motif (4 pieces)

14 cm (5 5/8")

12 cm (5")

9 cm (3 5/8"): 16 rows

43 cm (17")

54 cm (21 5/8")

21 Table Center

Materials: Anchor Mercer-Crochet no. 40 white, 20 g
Steel crochet hook no. 8 (size 0.9 mm)
Finished Size: A=37.5×25.5 cm (15×14″); B=17 cm (7″) square
Directions: A—Make motifs in numerical order. Ch 8, join with sl st to form ring, following chart, rows 1–5.

After row 4, cut off thread and attach thread to work row 5.

From second motif, while working row 5, join next motif with sl st.
B—Make and join 4 motifs, as for A, following chart. Work, joining motifs at center.

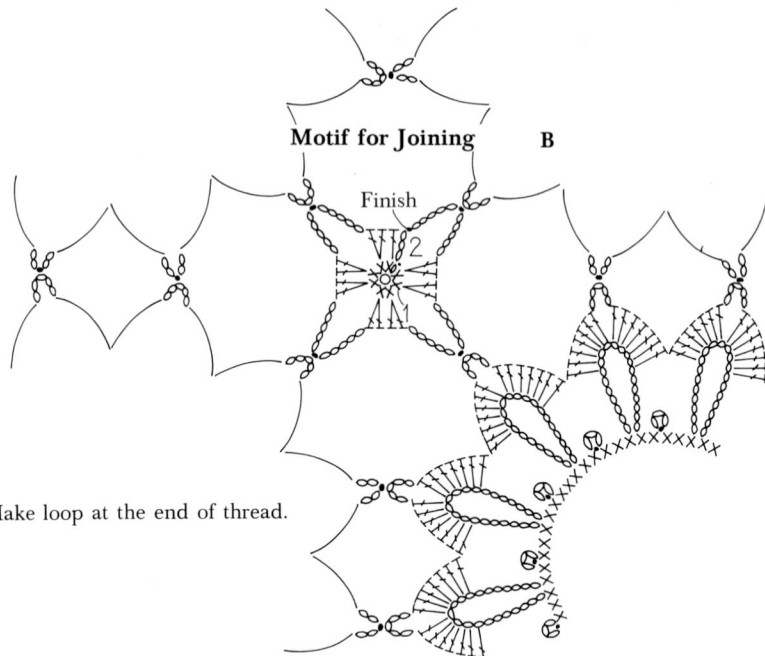

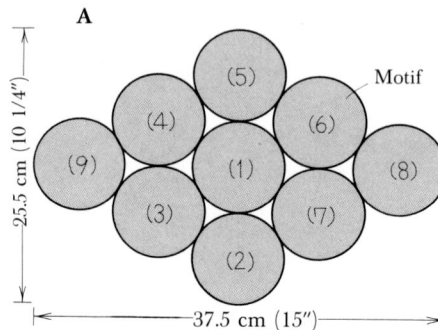

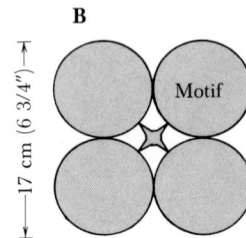

Motif for Joining   B

Finish

* Make loop at the end of thread.

A

25.5 cm (10 1/4″)

Motif

(9) (4) (5) (6) (8) (1) (3) (2) (7)

37.5 cm (15″)

B

17 cm (6 3/4″)

Motif

Motif for Joining   **A**

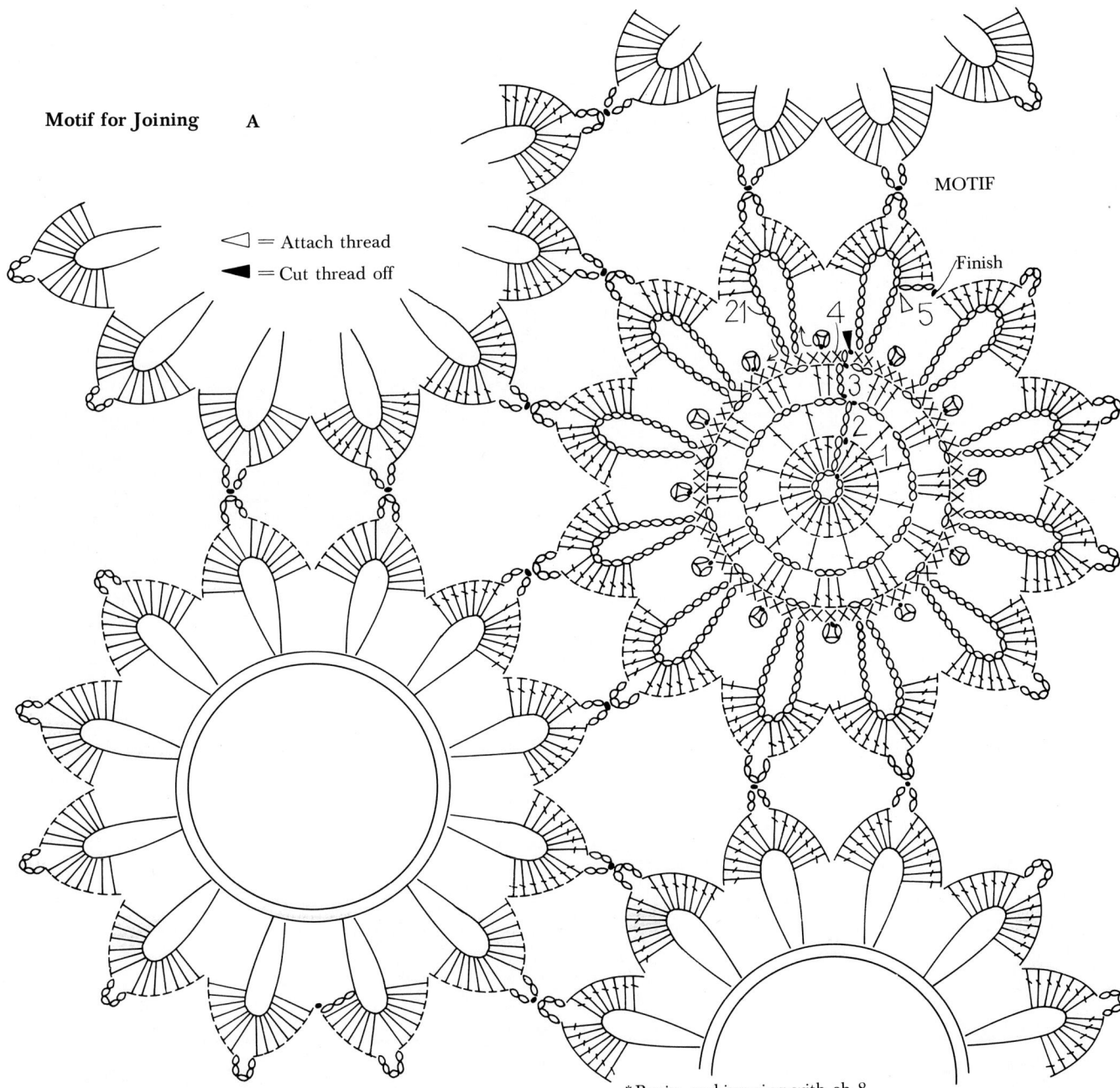

▷ = Attach thread

◀ = Cut thread off

MOTIF

Finish

21   4   5

3

2

1

8.5 cm (3 1/2")

*Begin, making ring with ch 8.

22 Rose Table Center

Materials: Anchor Mercer-Crochet no. 30 white, 60 g
Steel crochet hook no. 8 (size 0.9 mm)
Gauge: 10 cm (4″) = 61 st and 21 rows
Finished Size: 36 cm × 53.5 cm (14¼ × 21½″) oval
Directions: Beginning at center line, ch 190. Work in filet mesh, following chart, to row 30.

Decrease on right and left sides row 31–51.

Following chart, work opposite side in filet mesh from foundation chain to row 50. Work 4 rows edging, following chart.

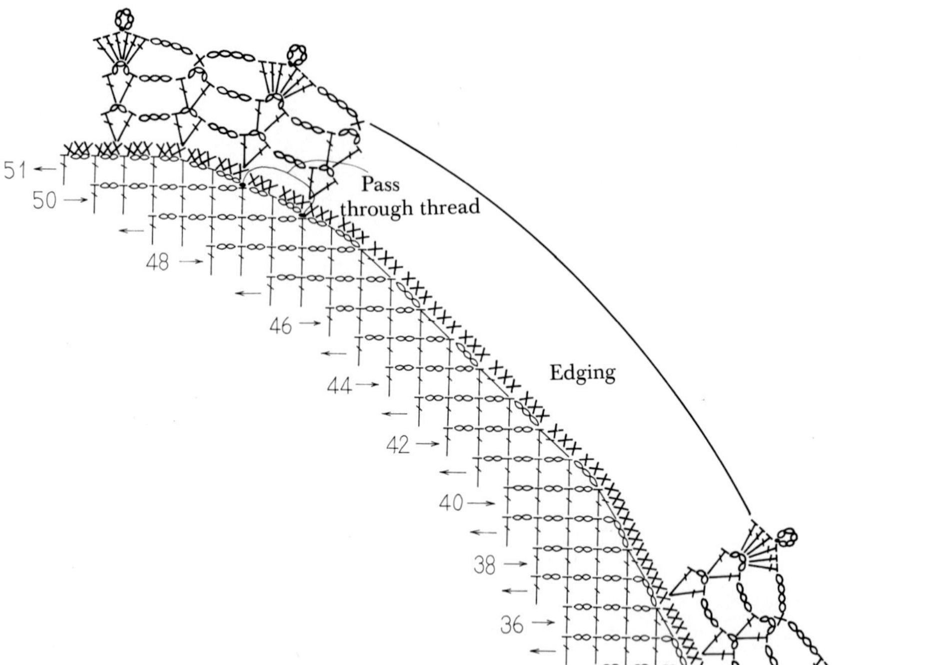

51
50
48
46
44
42
40
38
36
34
32
30
Pass through thread
Edging
1 pattern
4
2
1
1
2
3
Attach thread
1 2 3 4
Finish

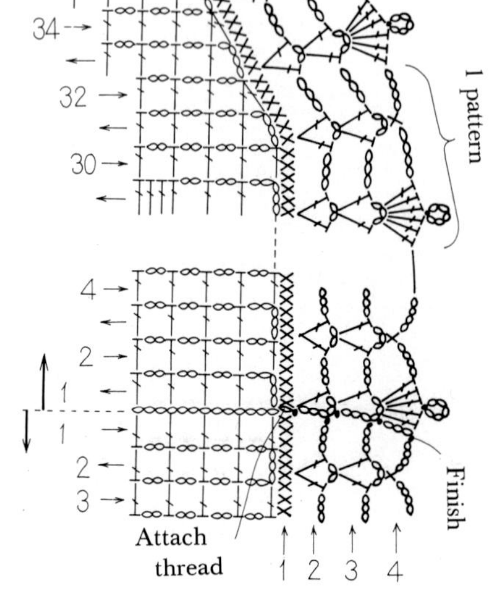

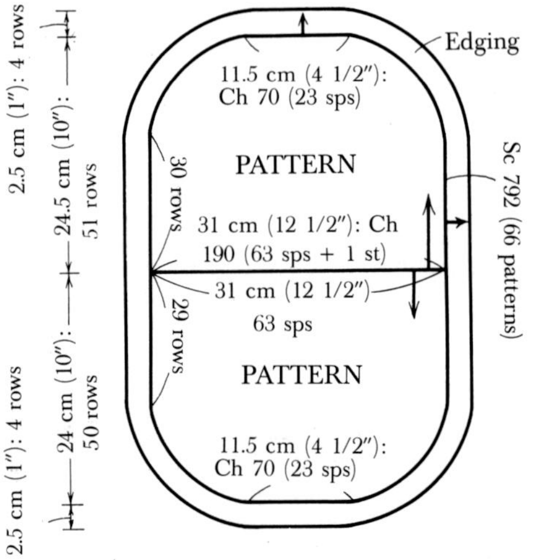

Edging
11.5 cm (4 1/2″): Ch 70 (23 sps)
PATTERN
30 rows
31 cm (12 1/2″): Ch 190 (63 sps + 1 st)
31 cm (12 1/2″)
63 sps
29 rows
PATTERN
11.5 cm (4 1/2″): Ch 70 (23 sps)
Sc 792 (66 patterns)
2.5 cm (1″): 4 rows
24.5 cm (10″): 51 rows
24 cm (10″): 50 rows
2.5 cm (1″): 4 rows

Filet Mesh Pattern Chart

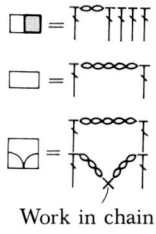

Legend:

- ▨ = pattern symbol (filled mesh)
- ▭ = pattern symbol (open mesh)
- ⊠ = pattern symbol

Work in chain

Center

mesh

23 Table Center

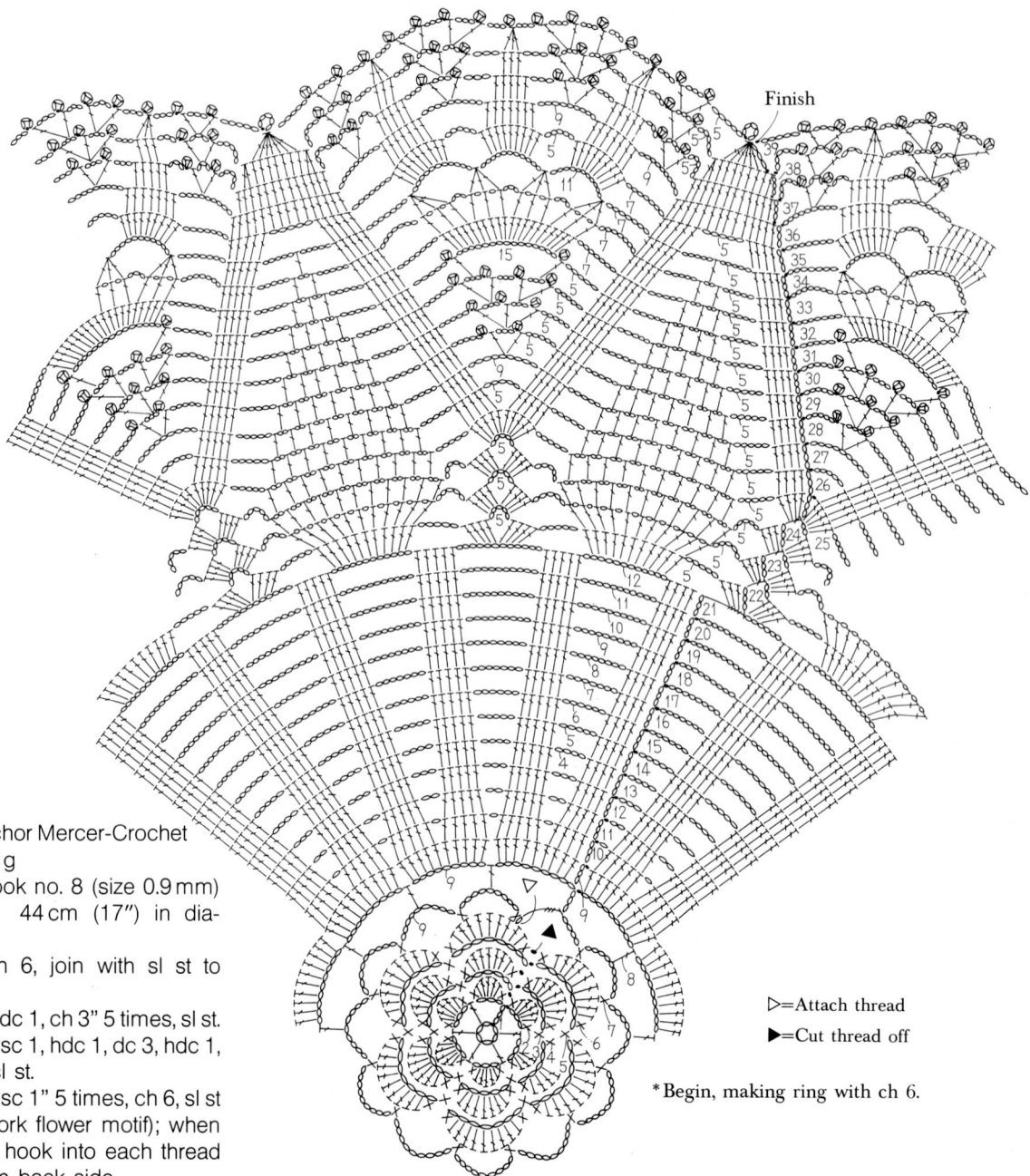

Finish

Materials: Anchor Mercer-Crochet no. 40 white, 50 g
Steel crochet hook no. 8 (size 0.9 mm)
Finished Size: 44 cm (17″) in diameter
Directions: Ch 6, join with sl st to form ring.
Row 1: Ch 6, "dc 1, ch 3" 5 times, sl st.
Row 2: Ch 1, "sc 1, hdc 1, dc 3, hdc 1, sc 1" 6 times, sl st.
Row 3: "Ch 6, sc 1" 5 times, ch 6, sl st (see p. 95 to work flower motif); when working sc, put hook into each thread of row 2 sc from back side.
Row 4: Ch 1, "sc 1, hdc 1, dc 5, hdc 1, sc 1" 6 times, sl st.
Row 5: "Ch 8, sc 1" 5 times, ch 8, sl st. Work sc in same manner as row 3.

Row 6: Ch 1, "sc 1, hdc 1, dc 7, hdc 1, sc 1" 6 times, sl st. Cut off thread.
Row 7–39: Attach thread at point indicated. Work, following chart.

▷=Attach thread
►=Cut thread off

*Begin, making ring with ch 6.

54

For Gifts

Coaster,
Cap,
Small purses,
Pincushions,
Potpourri Bags,
Handkerchiefs,
Collars,
and Pochettes

24 Coasters

Materials: Anchor Mercer-Crochet no. 30 white, 5 g

Steel crochet hook no. 8 (size 0.9 mm)

Finished Size: 14 cm (5½″) in diameter

Directions: Ch 8, join sl st to form ring.

Row 1: Ch 3, dc 23 in ring.

Row 2–14: Follow chart.

Row 10–14: While increasing the number of chain stitches, work in mesh pattern.

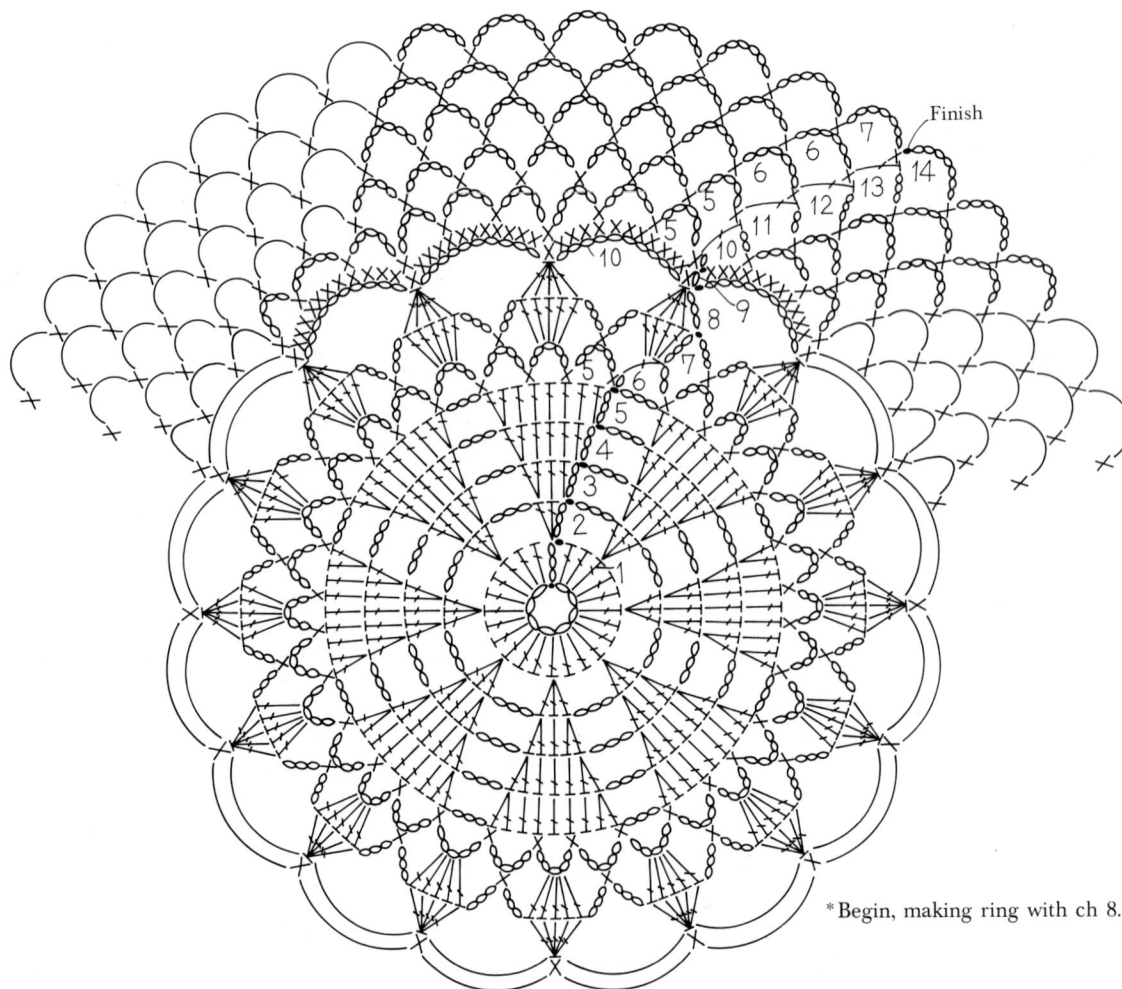

Finish

*Begin, making ring with ch 8.

25 Bottle Caps

Materials: Anchor Mercer-Crochet no. 30 light blue, 5 g; lavender, 5 g; pink, 5 g Steel crochet hook no. 8 (size 0.9 mm); 50 cm (20″) length of 6 mm (¼″)-wide satin ribbon.

Finished Size: 13 cm (5″) in diameter

Directions: Make loop at end of thread.

Row 1: Ch 5, "hdc 1, ch 3" 4 times in loop.

Row 2–21: Follow chart.

Rows 3, 5, 7, and 9: Work chain on back side of preceding row (see p. 95).

From row 10, while increasing number of chains, work in mesh pattern. Fit to bottle size, pass ribbon through part of net, and tie.

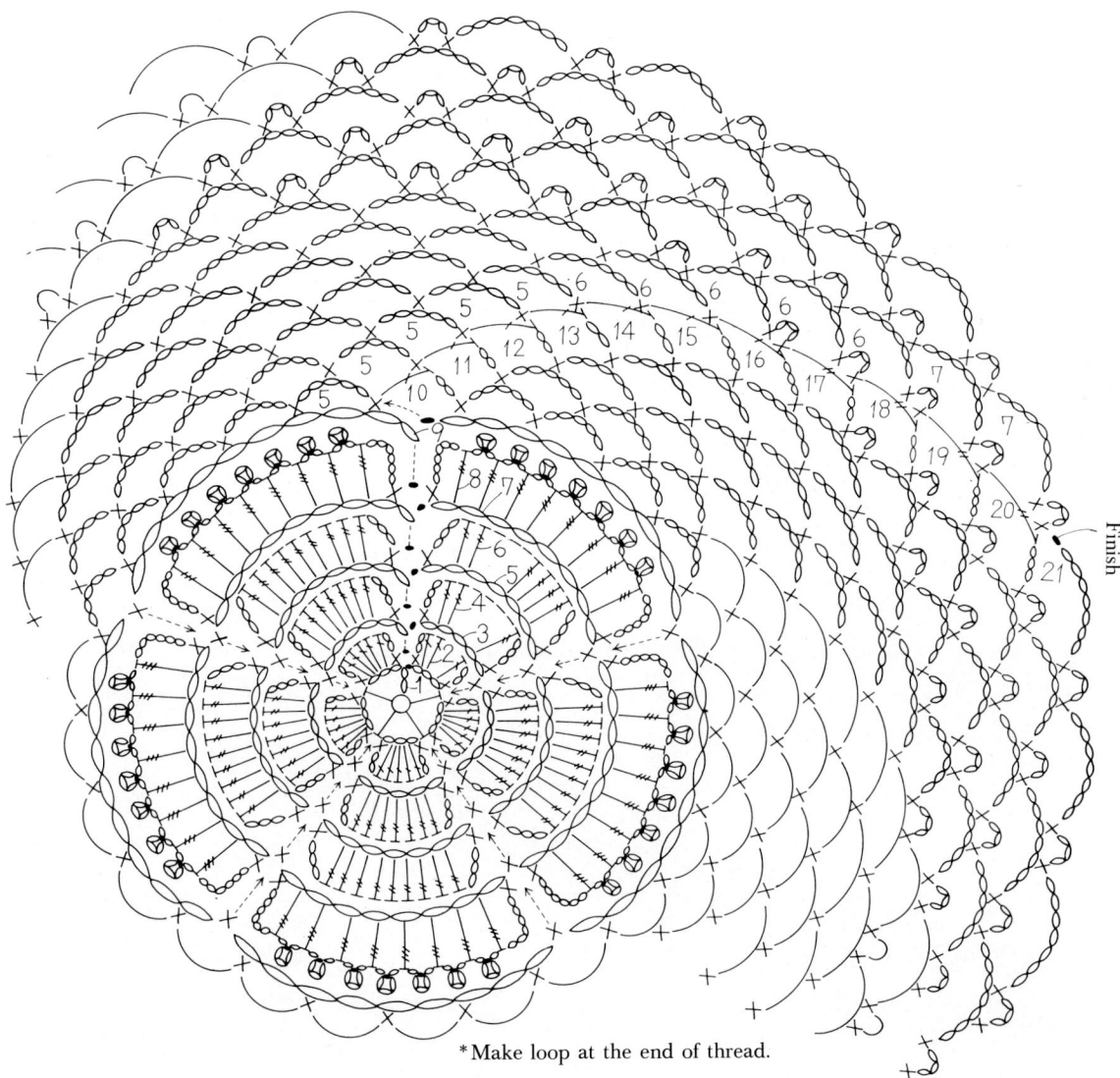

*Make loop at the end of thread.

26 Small Purses

A Purse

Materials: Anchor Mercer-Crochet no. 40 white, 5 g
Steel crochet hook no. 8 (size 0.9 mm); 14×32 cm (5½×12½″) pieces each of small floral cotton print and thin padding; 50 cm (20″) length of 1.5 cm (⅛″) pink satin ribbon; 1 pair snap fasteners.

Finished Size: 12 cm (4¾″) square

Directions: Attach thin padding to wrong side of cotton. Cut to indicated size, adding 1 cm (⅜″) for seam allowance (except add 1.5 cm (⅝″) around flap).

Following chart, work lace and ruffles on both sides. Pass ribbon through center of lace and sew center to case with tiny slip stitches. Attach snap fasteners and tie ribbon.

B Purse

Materials: Anchor Mercer-Crochet no. 40 white, 5 g
Steel crochet hook no. 8 (size 0.9 mm); 10×22 cm (4×9″) pieces of floral cotton print and thin padding; 40 cm (16″) length of 6 mm (¼″)-wide pink satin ribbon; 1 pair small snap fasteners.

Finished Size: 8 cm (3¼″) square

Directions: Follow directions for A.

A and B Small Purses

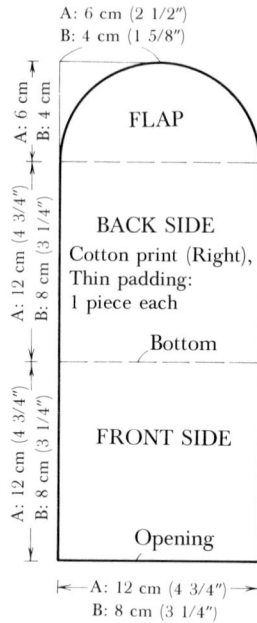

A: 6 cm (2 1/2″)
B: 4 cm (1 5/8″)

A: 6 cm
B: 4 cm

FLAP

BACK SIDE
Cotton print (Right),
Thin padding:
1 piece each

Bottom

A: 12 cm (4 3/4″)
B: 8 cm (3 1/4″)

FRONT SIDE

A: 12 cm (4 3/4″)
B: 8 cm (3 1/4″)

Opening

A: 12 cm (4 3/4″)
B: 8 cm (3 1/4″)

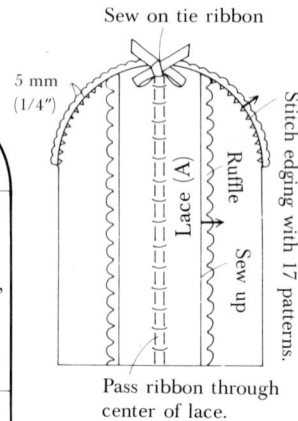

Sew on tie ribbon
5 mm (1/4″)
Lace (A)
Ruffle
Sew up
Stitch edging with 17 patterns.

Pass ribbon through center of lace.

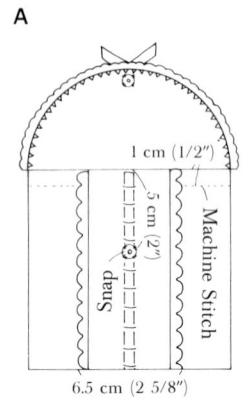

A
1 cm (1/2″)
5 cm (2″)
Snap
Machine Stitch
6.5 cm (2 5/8″)

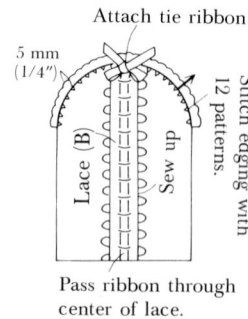

Attach tie ribbon
5 mm (1/4″)
Lace (B)
Sew up
Stitch edging with 12 patterns.

Pass ribbon through center of lace.

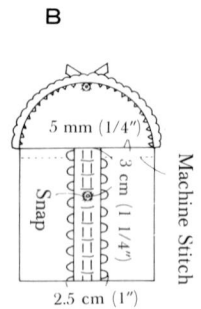

B
5 mm (1/4″)
3 cm (1 1/4″)
Snap
Machine Stitch
2.5 cm (1″)

Lace A

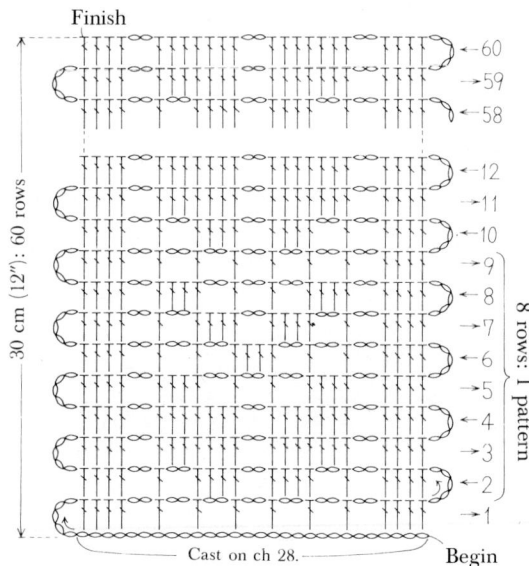

Finish

30 cm (12″): 60 rows

8 rows: 1 pattern

—60
—59
—58
—12
—11
—10
—9
—8
—7
—6
—5
—4
—3
—2
—1

Cast on ch 28.

Begin

Lace B

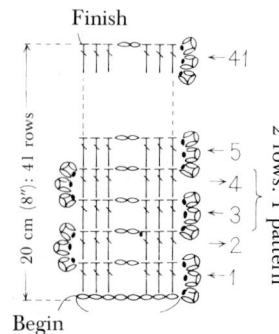

Finish

20 cm (8″): 41 rows

2 rows: 1 pattern

—41
—5
—4
—3
—2
—1

Begin

Edging

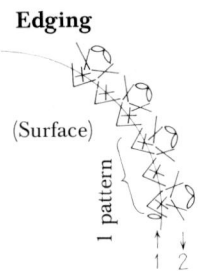

(Surface)

1 pattern

1 2

Ruffle

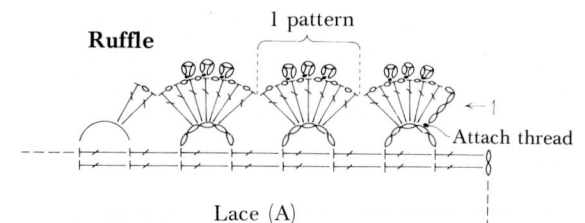

1 pattern

Attach thread

Lace (A)

27 Small Purses

Pencil Cases

Materials: Anchor Mercer-Crochet no. 40 white, 5 g

Steel crochet hook no. 8 (size 0.9 mm); 20×11 cm (8×4⅜″) pieces of small floral cotton print and thin padding; 18 cm (7″) zipper.

Finished Size: 4.5×18 cm (1⅞×7⅛″)

Directions: Attach thin pad to wrong side of cotton print and cut it out, adding 1 cm (⅜″) seam allowance.

Attach zipper, sew both sides, turn to right side and attach lace with tiny slip stitches.

Small Bag

Materials: Anchor Mercer-Crochet no. 40 white, 5 g

Steel crochet hook no. 8 (size 0.9 mm); 30×22 cm (12×9″) pieces of small floral cotton print and thin padding; 50 cm (20″) length of 6 mm (¼″)-wide satin ribbon.

Finished Size: 13×18 cm (5×7⅛″)

Directions: Attach thin padding to wrong side of fabric, allowing 1 cm (⅜″) seam allowance, and make bag. Applique lace and ribbon on front. Braid 3 pieces of crochet cotton no. 40 for string, making 2 strings: 38 cm (15″) lengths, and pass drawstrings through top of bag. Leave 3 cm (1¼″) free at each end of braid for fringe.

Pencil Case

Cotton print, Thin padding: 2 pieces each

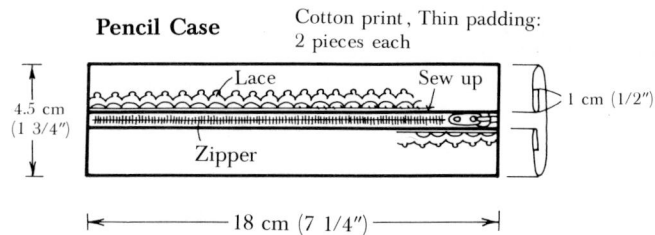

4.5 cm (1 3/4″)

18 cm (7 1/4″)

1 cm (1/2″)

Lace

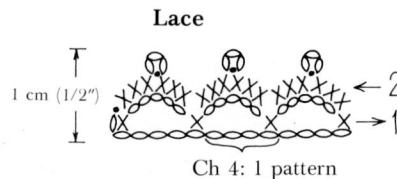

1 cm (1/2″)

Ch 4: 1 pattern

★ 2 pieces: 23 patterns each

Small Bag

Cotton print, Thin padding: 1 piece each

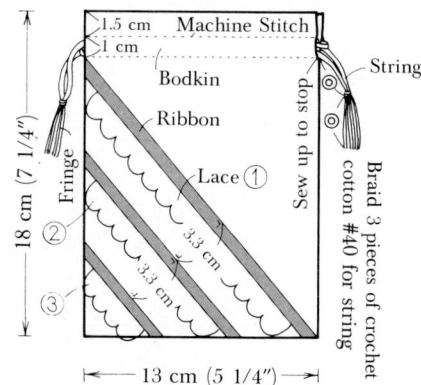

18 cm (7 1/4″)

13 cm (5 1/4″)

①: 14 patterns   ②: 9 patterns
③: 4 patterns

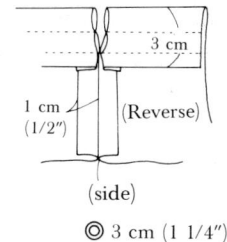

3 cm

1 cm (1/2″)   (Reverse)

(side)

◎ 3 cm (1 1/4″)

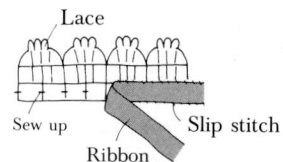

Lace

Sew up   Ribbon   Slip stitch

Lace

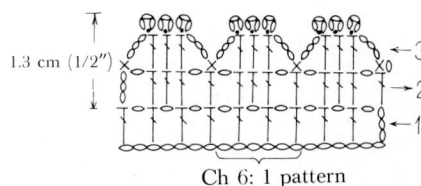

1.3 cm (1/2″)

Ch 6: 1 pattern

28 Pincushion

Materials: Anchor Mercer-Crochet no. 30 white, 5 g; pink, 5 g
Steel crochet hook no. 8 (size 0.9 mm); 18 × 9 cm (7⅛ × 3½″) floral cotton print; 7 cm (2⅛″) square of ready-made cotton lace.

Finished Size: 10 cm (4″) square

Directions: Cut 2 pieces of cotton, adding 1 cm (⅜″) seam allowance.
Sew cotton lace on front; make 7 cm (2¾″) square cushion.

Work edging of A and B; attach crocheted flower motif at center.

A Pincushion

1.5 cm (5/8″)

7 cm (2 3/4″)

Edging B

Edging A

Cloth

Small flower

Flower

Lace

1 cm (3/8″)

1.2 cm (1/2″)

Cloth

Lace

Cloth

Sew up

Slip stitch

Flower (White)

2.8 cm (1 1/8″)

Finish

4
3
2
1

Small flower (Pink)

1.3 cm (1/2″)

Finish

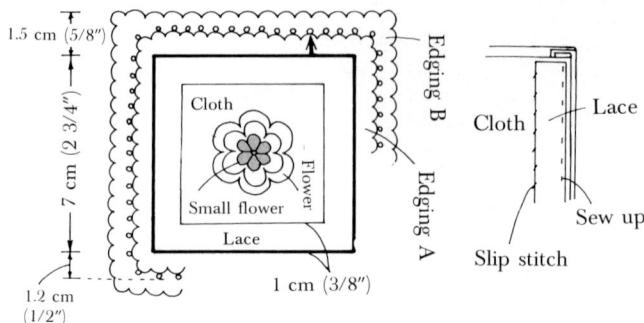

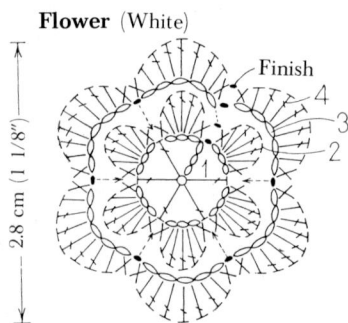

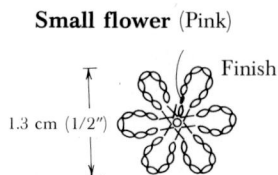

*Make loop at the end of thread.

Edging A. (White)

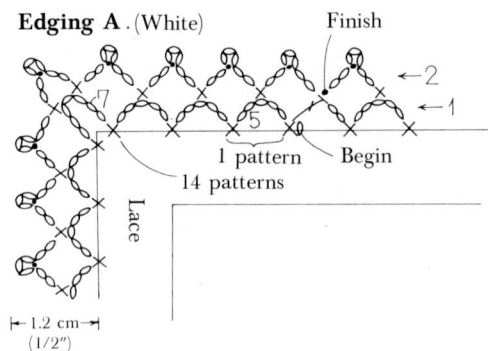

Finish

2
1

7

5

1 pattern

Begin

14 patterns

Lace

1.2 cm (1/2″)

Edging B (White)

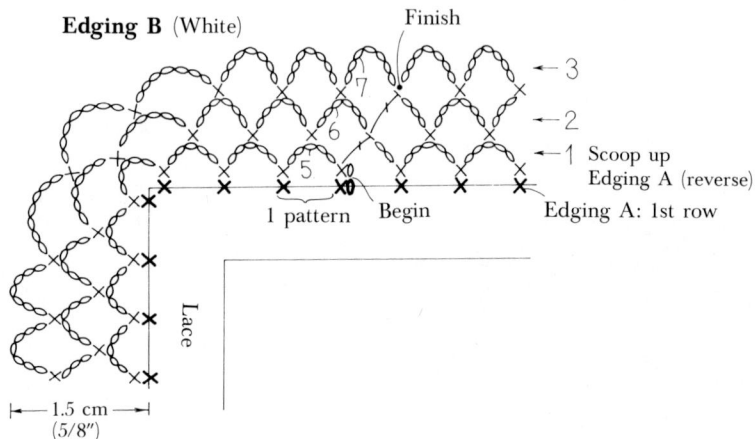

Finish

3
2
1 Scoop up
Edging A (reverse)

7

6

5

1 pattern

Begin

Edging A: 1st row

Lace

1.5 cm (5/8″)

29 Pinsuchion and Bag

Pincushion

Materials: Anchor Mercer-Crochet no. 30 cream, 5 g
Steel crochet hook no. 8 (size 0.9 mm); 12×20 cm (5×8″) piece of floral cotton; 40 cm (16″) length of 6 mm (¼″)-wide yellow-green satin ribbon; 7 cm (2¾″) square thick paper; some chemical wad
Finished Size: 9 cm (3½″) diameter
Directions: Cut thick paper to indicated size; cut cotton, adding 1 cm (⅜″) seam allowance.

Baste loosely around fabric and pull the thread, putting paper in bottom of cotton. Stuff chemical wad into upper cotton.

Put bottom and top together and edging in between; stitch all around with tiny slip stitches. Attach ribbon and tie.

Potpourri Bag

Materials: Anchor Mercer-Crochet no. 30 white, 5 g; light blue, 5 g
Steel crochet hook no. 8 (size 0.9 mm); 21×10 cm (8¼×4″) piece of light blue linen; 20 cm (8″) length of 6 mm (¼″)-wide blue satin ribbon; potpourri.
Finished Size: 10 cm (4″) square
Directions: Cut linen, adding 1 cm (⅜″) seam allowance.

Make opening on back. With right sides of front and back together, stitch all around. Turn to right side. Work edging, following chart. Sew ribbon and motif onto front. Stuff with potpourri and close with slip stitches.

B Pincushion

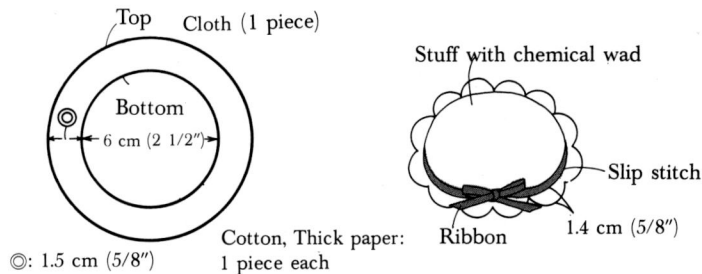

Edging

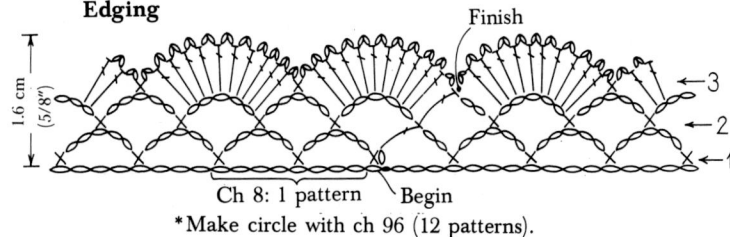

*Make circle with ch 96 (12 patterns).

C Potpourri Bag

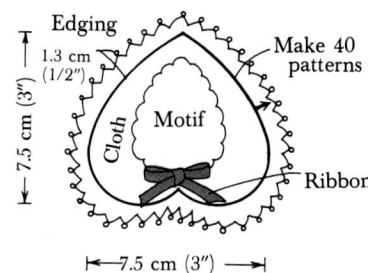

Motif (White)

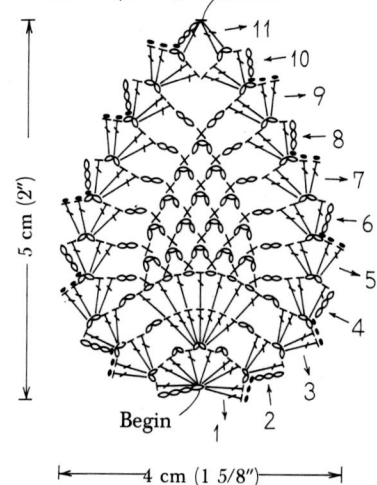

Edging (Blue)

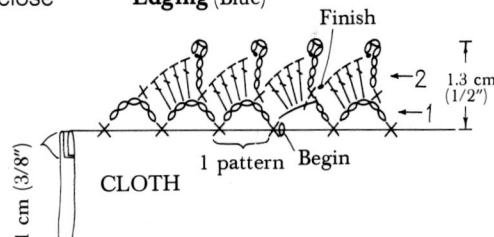

30 Potpourri Bags

Materials: Anchor Mercer-Crochet no. 30 light blue, 5 g

Steel crochet hook no. 8 (size 0.9 mm); 21 × 13 cm (8¼ × 5″) piece of floral cotton print; ready-made square of 5.5 cm (2″) flower lace; 40 cm (16″) length of 6 mm (¼″)-wide cream satin ribbon; potpourri.

Finished Size: 12.5 × 9.5 cm (5 × 3¾″)

Directions: Cut out cotton, adding 1 cm (⅜″) seam allowance at bottom and side, and 5 mm (¼″) on open side. Attach lace motif and crocheted cord (see p. 98) to front of bag; sew bottom and sides. Shirr at place indicated. Put potpourri in bag and attach tied ribbon.

Materials: Anchor Mercer-Crochet no. 30 white, 5 g; lavender, 5 g

Steel crochet hook no. 8 (size 0.9 mm); 11 × 17 cm (4¼ × 7″) piece of small floral cotton print; potpourri.

Finished Size: 7.5 × 11 cm (3 × 4¼″)

Directions: Make bag in same manner as D, following chart.

Work flowers A and B and attach them to front.

Make a string of crocheted cord (see p. 98) and add a 7-dc puff at both ends of cord. Put potpourri in bag and tie closed.

D Potpourri Bag

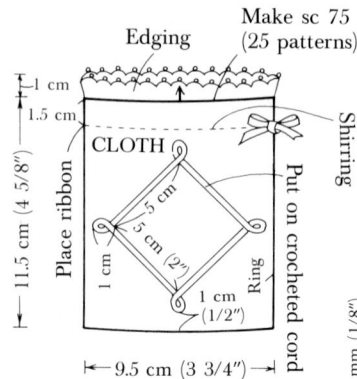

String (Violet)

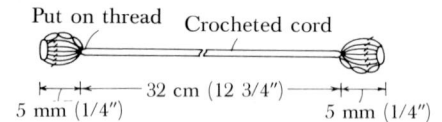

Edging

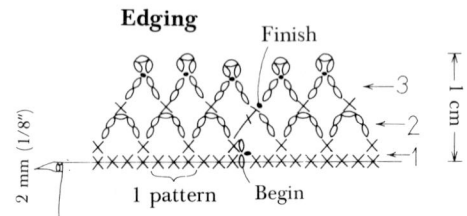

E Potpourri Bag

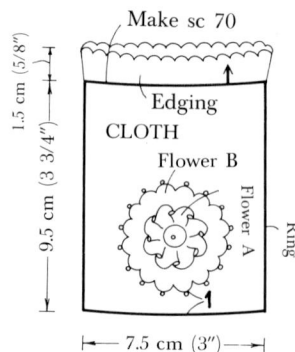

Edging

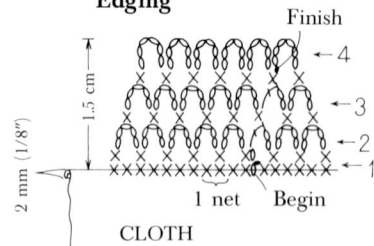

Flower B

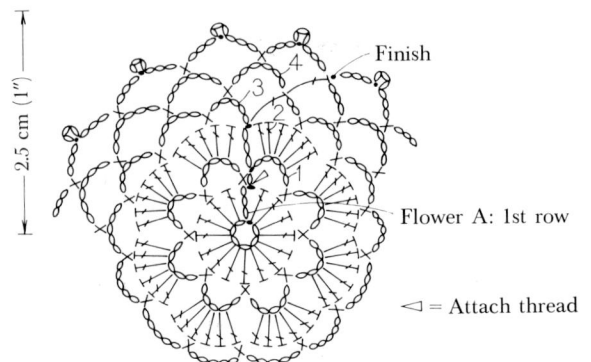

Flower A: 1st row

◁ = Attach thread

Flower A

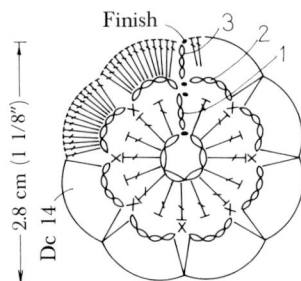

*Begin, making ring with ch 6.

31 Potpourri Bag

Materials: Anchor Mercer-Crochet no. 30 white, 10 g; light blue, 9 g; lavender, 5 g; violet, 5 g
Steel crochet hooks no. 8 and no. 2 (sizes 0.9 and 1.5 mm); 4.8×3.5 cm (2×1½″) ribbon-shaped lace; potpourri.
Finished Size: 10.5×11 cm (4×4½″)
Directions: With no. 8 hook, work front and back (wrong sides together), following chart. While working edging A, close 3 sides. Work edging B on open side. Sew ribbon-shaped lace on front. Work 3 small flowers, 1 in each color, and appliqué on front. Work string of 2 strands with no. 2 hook.

F Potpourri Bag

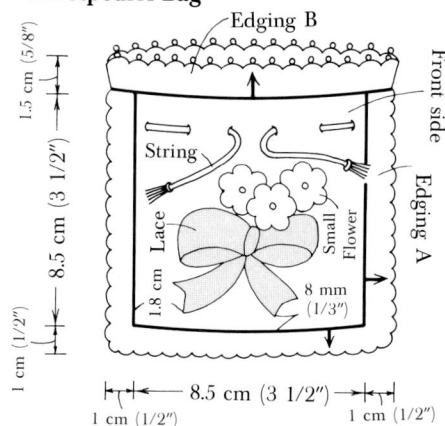

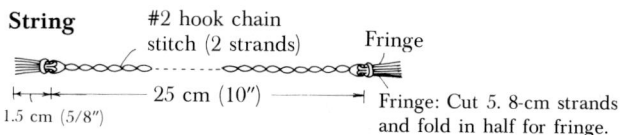

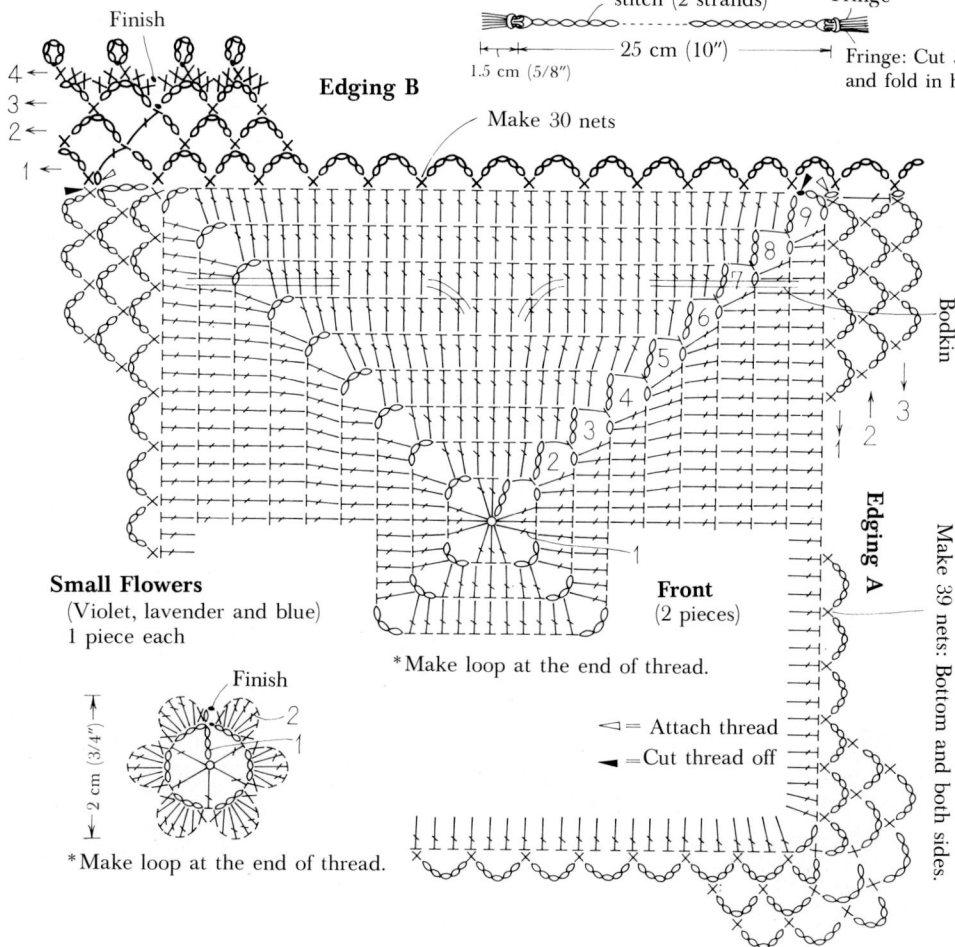

Edging B

1.5 cm (5/8″)

Front side

String

Edging A

8.5 cm (3 1/2″)

1.8 cm Lace

Small Flower

8 mm (1/3″)

1 cm (1/2″)

8.5 cm (3 1/2″)

1 cm (1/2″)   1 cm (1/2″)

String   #2 hook chain stitch (2 strands)   Fringe

25 cm (10″)

1.5 cm (5/8″)   Fringe: Cut 5. 8-cm strands and fold in half for fringe.

Finish

Edging B

4 ←
3 ←
2 ←
1 ←

Make 30 nets

Bodkin

Make 39 nets: Bottom and both sides.

Edging A

Small Flowers
(Violet, lavender and blue)
1 piece each

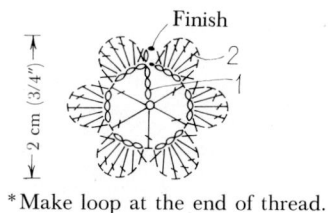

Finish

2 cm (3/4″)

*Make loop at the end of thread.

Front
(2 pieces)

*Make loop at the end of thread.

▷ = Attach thread
◀ = Cut thread off

Materials: Anchor Mercer-Crochet no. 40 white, 5 g
Steel crochet hook no. 8 (size 0.9 mm); white lawn 27 cm (11″) square.
Finished Size: 25.5 cm (10″) square.
Directions: Work in same manner as B, p. 73; cut out cloth and work edging. Following diagram, cut out one corner of cloth, adding 3 mm (1/8″) seam allowance; turn to right side and baste. Work and attach motif, following diagram.

A Handkerchief

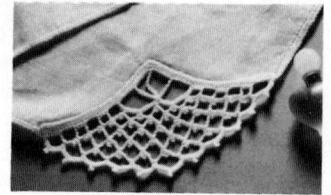

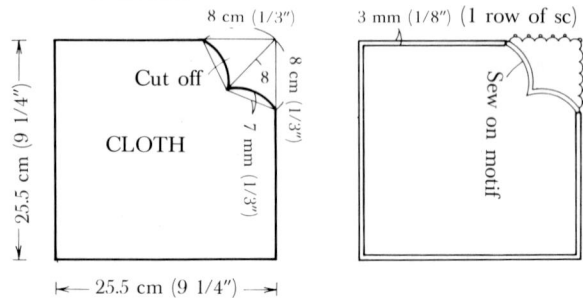

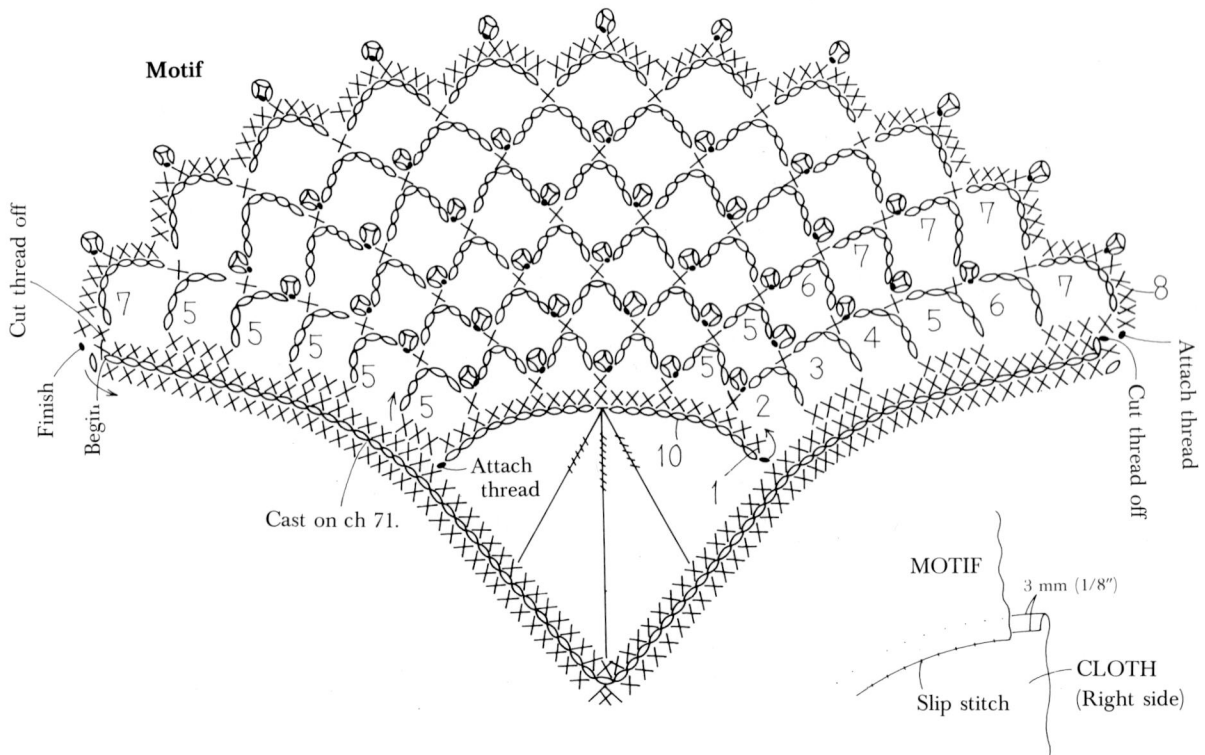

8 cm (1/3″)

8 cm (1/3″)

8

Cut off

7 mm (1/3″)

25.5 cm (9 1/4″)

CLOTH

25.5 cm (9 1/4″)

3 mm (1/8″) (1 row of sc)

Sew on motif

Motif

Cut thread off

Finish

Begin

7

5

5

5

5

5

5

Cast on ch 71.

Attach thread

10

1

2

3

4

6

5

6

7

7

7

7

8

Attach thread

Cut thread off

MOTIF

3 mm (1/8″)

CLOTH
(Right side)

Slip stitch

33 Handkerchief

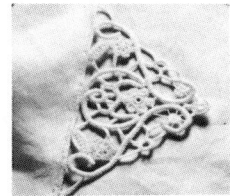

Materials: Anchor Mercer-Crochet no. 40 white, 10 g
Steel crochet hook no. 8 (size 0.9 mm)
Finished Size: 25.5 cm (10″) square
Directions: Cut out cloth of indicated size along grain of fabric, adding 3 mm (⅛″) seam allowance, and cut out one corner.

Pull two threads 5 mm (¼″) in from edge, fold in half and work sc around cloth, inserting hook into line of pulled threads. At cut corner, work sc along a rolled 3 mm (⅛″) allowance.

Trace design on paper and put A–E motifs on it.

Work buttonhole bridge and spider web stitches in spaces (see p. 98). Attach lace at cut corner.

B Handkerchief

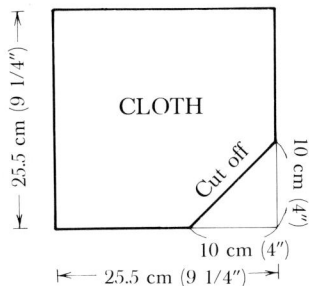

CLOTH

25.5 cm (9 1/4″)

10 cm (4″)

Cut off

10 cm (4″)

25.5 cm (9 1/4″)

Buttonhole bridge

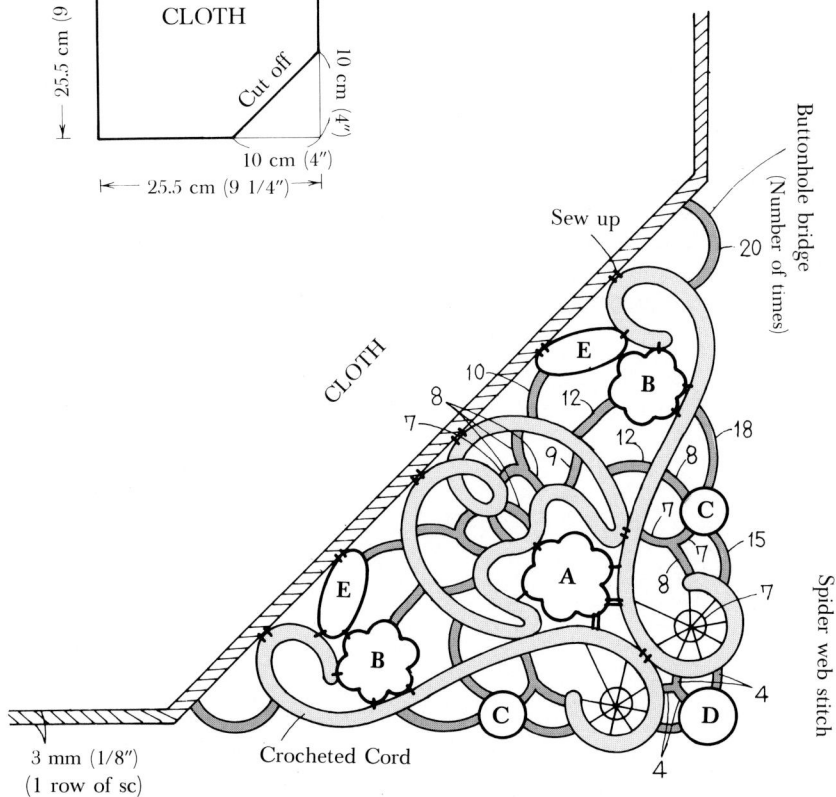

Sew up

Buttonhole bridge (Number of times)

20

CLOTH

10

E

B

12

8

7

12

18

9

8

C

7

E

A

7

15

B

8

7

C

D

4

Spider web stitch

4

3 mm (1/8″)
(1 row of sc)

Crocheted Cord

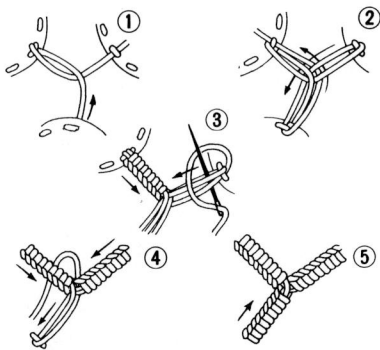

A (1 piece)

Finish

*Make loop at the end of thread.

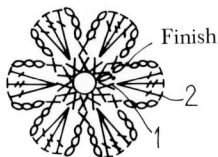

B (2 pieces)

Finish

2

1

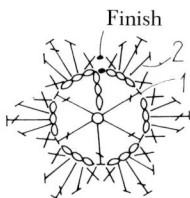

C (2 pieces)

Finish

*Begin, making ring with ch 10.

D (1 piece)

Finish

*Make loop at the end of thread.

E (2 pieces)

Finish

2

1

Cast on ch 11.

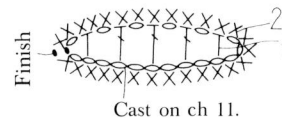

C, D, and E Handerkerchiefs

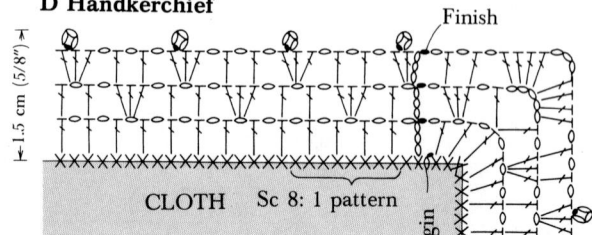

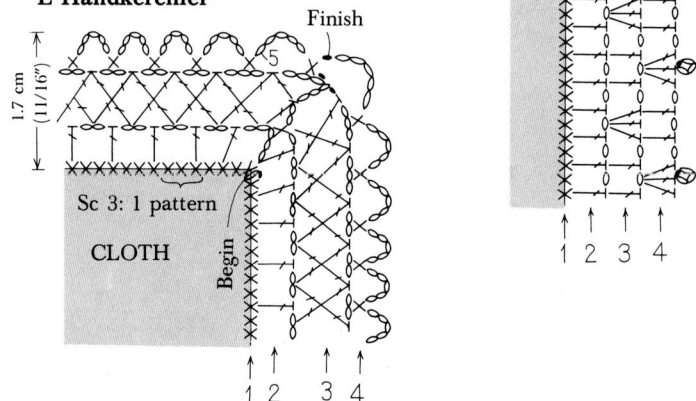

Materials: Anchor Mercer-Crochet no. 40 white, 20 g each for C, D, and E Steel crochet hook no. 8 (size 0.9 mm); 2 handkerchiefs 41 cm (16¼") square for D and E; 26 cm (10¼") square of lawn for C.

Finished Size: C=30.5 cm (12") square; D and E=approx. 44 cm (17¼") square

Directions: D and E: Following chart, work 4 rows of edging.

C: Cut cloth along grain, pull threads 5 mm (¼") from edge and fold in half. Work sc along it, following chart, and work 5 rows of edging.

C Handkerchief

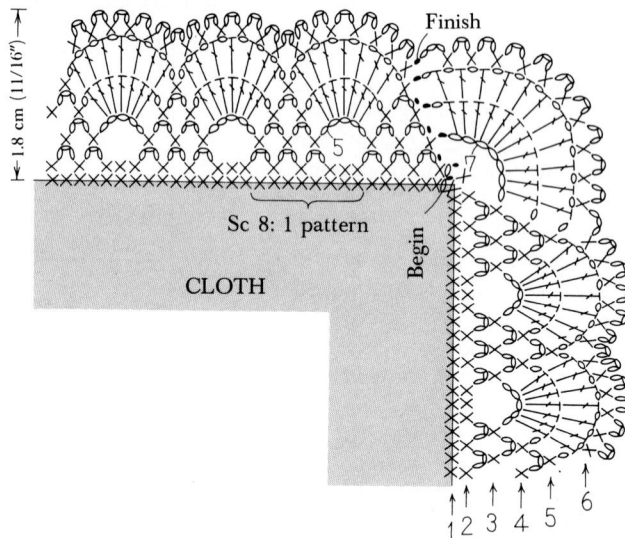

1.8 cm (11/16")

Finish

Sc 8: 1 pattern

CLOTH

Begin

1 2 3 4 5 6

D Handkerchief

1.5 cm (5/8")

Finish

CLOTH   Sc 8: 1 pattern

Begin

1 2 3 4

E Handkerchief

1.7 cm (11/16")

Finish

5

Sc 3: 1 pattern

CLOTH

Begin

1 2 3 4

35 Pochette

Materials: Anchor Mercer-Crochet no. 30 brown, 50 g
Steel crochet hook no. 8 (size 0.9 mm); 45×25 cm (18×10″) pieces of dark green linen and a beige fabric; 17.5 cm (7″) zipper.
Finished Size: 20×15 cm (8×6″)
Directions: Cut fabrics, adding 1 cm (½″) seam allowance.

Make base, flowers, leaves, and crocheted cords (see p. 98), following chart, and sew them on front. Sew linen and lining separately; attach zipper on open side. Using crochet cotton, make 3 lengths of braid 200 cm (80″) long, leaving an unbraided fringe at each end.

Cutting and Appliqué Diagram

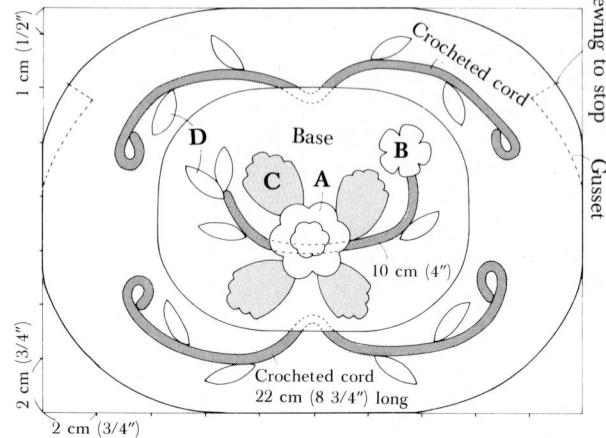

Gusset: 3 cm (1 1/4″), wide × 39 cm (15 5/8″) long

Front, Gusset
Right, Reverse: 2 pieces each

Base

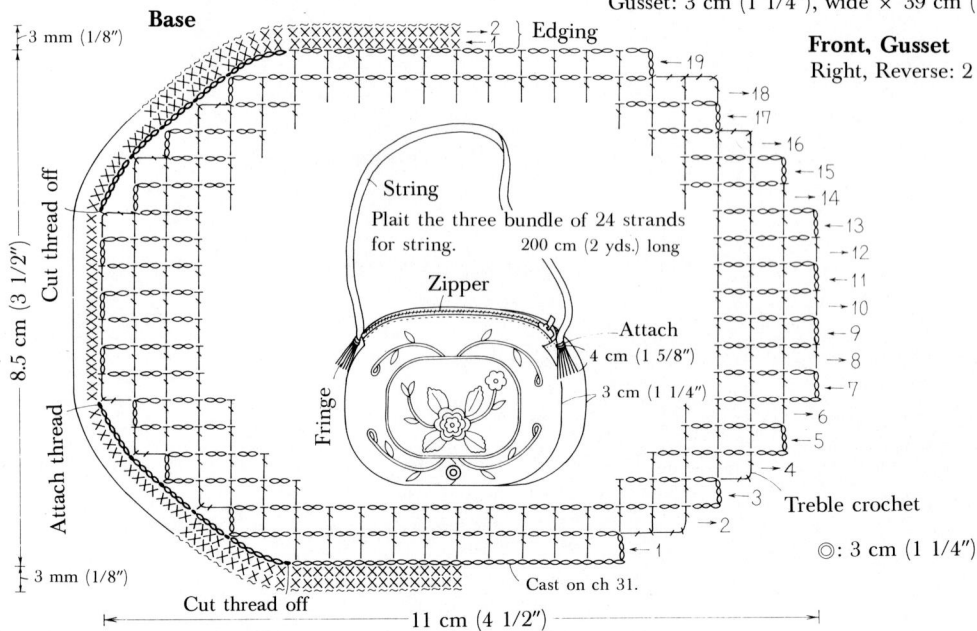

Treble crochet

◎: 3 cm (1 1/4″)

Flower

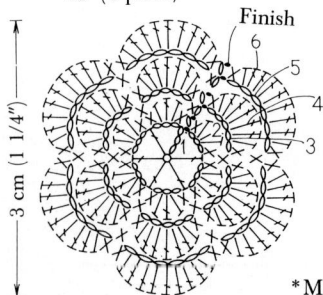

A (1 piece)

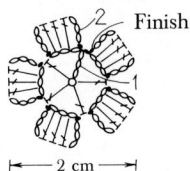

B (1 piece)

*Make loop at the end of thread.

Leaf

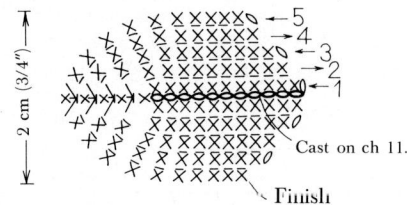

C (4 pieces)

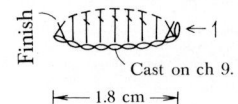

D (12 pieces)

36 Collar

Materials: Anchor Mercer-Crochet no. 5 (387), 40 g
Steel crochet hook no. 2 (size 1.5 mm)
Finished Size: 51 cm (20″) on neck size, 7.5 cm (3″) wide
Directions: Begin at edge of collar. Work to center back (row 28), following chart; cut thread off. Work other side and connect two points with sl st.

Work triangle part of back, following chart. Finish by working edging on outside of collar and dc on neck side.

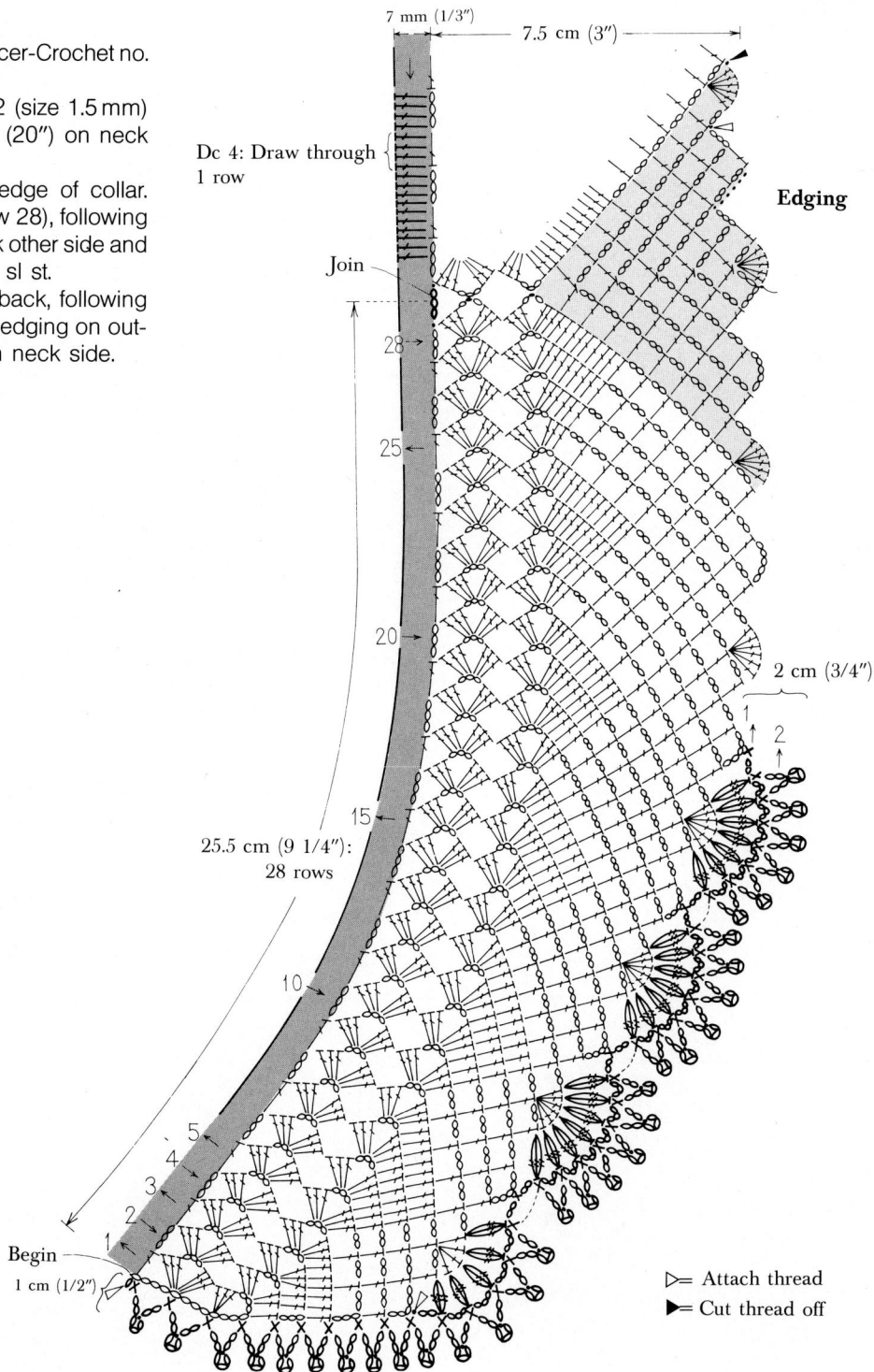

7 mm (1/3″)

7.5 cm (3″)

Dc 4: Draw through 1 row

Edging

Join

28

25

20

2 cm (3/4″)

1
2

15

25.5 cm (9 1/4″): 28 rows

10

5
4
3
2
1

Begin

1 cm (1/2″)

▷= Attach thread
►= Cut thread off

37
38
39

37 Collar

Materials: Anchor Mercer-Crochet no. 10 white, 40 g
Steel crochet hooks no. 4 and no. 2 (sizes 1.25 and 1.5 mm).
Finished Size: 50 cm (20″) on neck side, 9.5 cm (3¾″) wide
Directions: Following chart, increase one repeat and spread outer line. Work edging A at first, and work edging B continually. With sc and sl, make crocheted cord 85 cm (33½″) and pass through row 1.

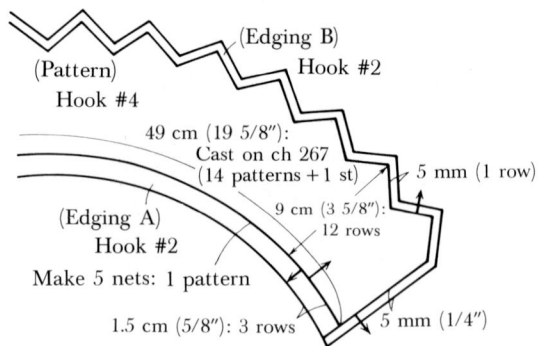

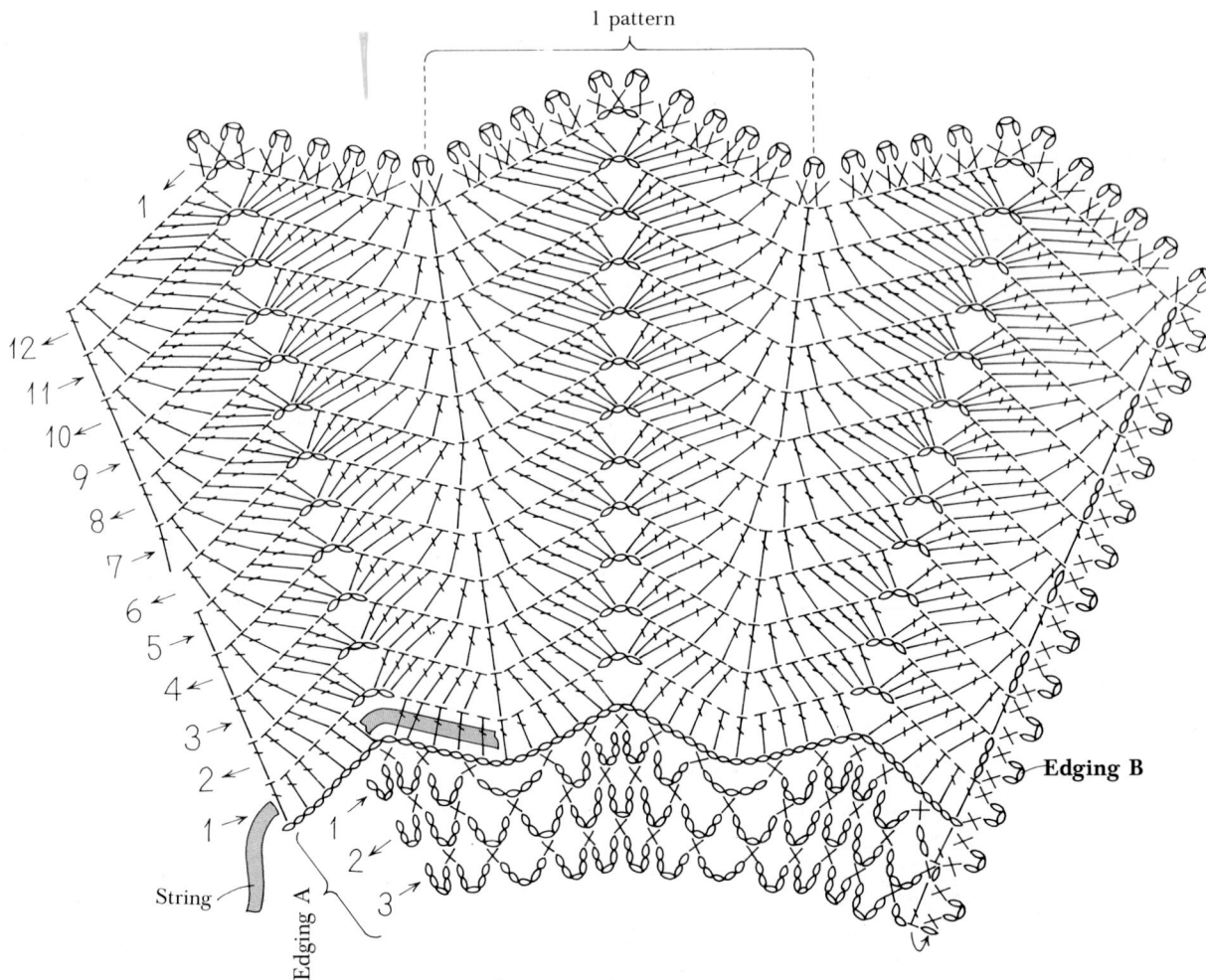

(Pattern)
Hook #4

(Edging B)
Hook #2

49 cm (19 5/8″):
Cast on ch 267
(14 patterns + 1 st)

5 mm (1 row)

(Edging A)
Hook #2

9 cm (3 5/8″):
12 rows

Make 5 nets: 1 pattern

1.5 cm (5/8″): 3 rows

5 mm (1/4″)

1 pattern

String

Edging A

Edging B

★ Cast on ch 19: 1 pattern

38 Collar

Materials: Anchor Mercer-Crochet no. 40 white, 60 g
Steel crochet hook no. 8 (size 0.9 mm); 1 m (39″) length of 5 mm (¼″)-wide ivory ribbon.
Gauge: 1 repeat of pattern A, beginning=1 cm (⅜″), end=3.5 cm (1⅜″)
Finished Size: 45 cm (17¾″) on neck side, 15 cm (5⅞″) wide
Directions: Ch 271 at neck side; work in pattern A and increase, following chart, to row 24.
Work in B pattern on neck side. Work sc 1 row on neck side and on both sides. Pass ribbon through first row of pattern A.

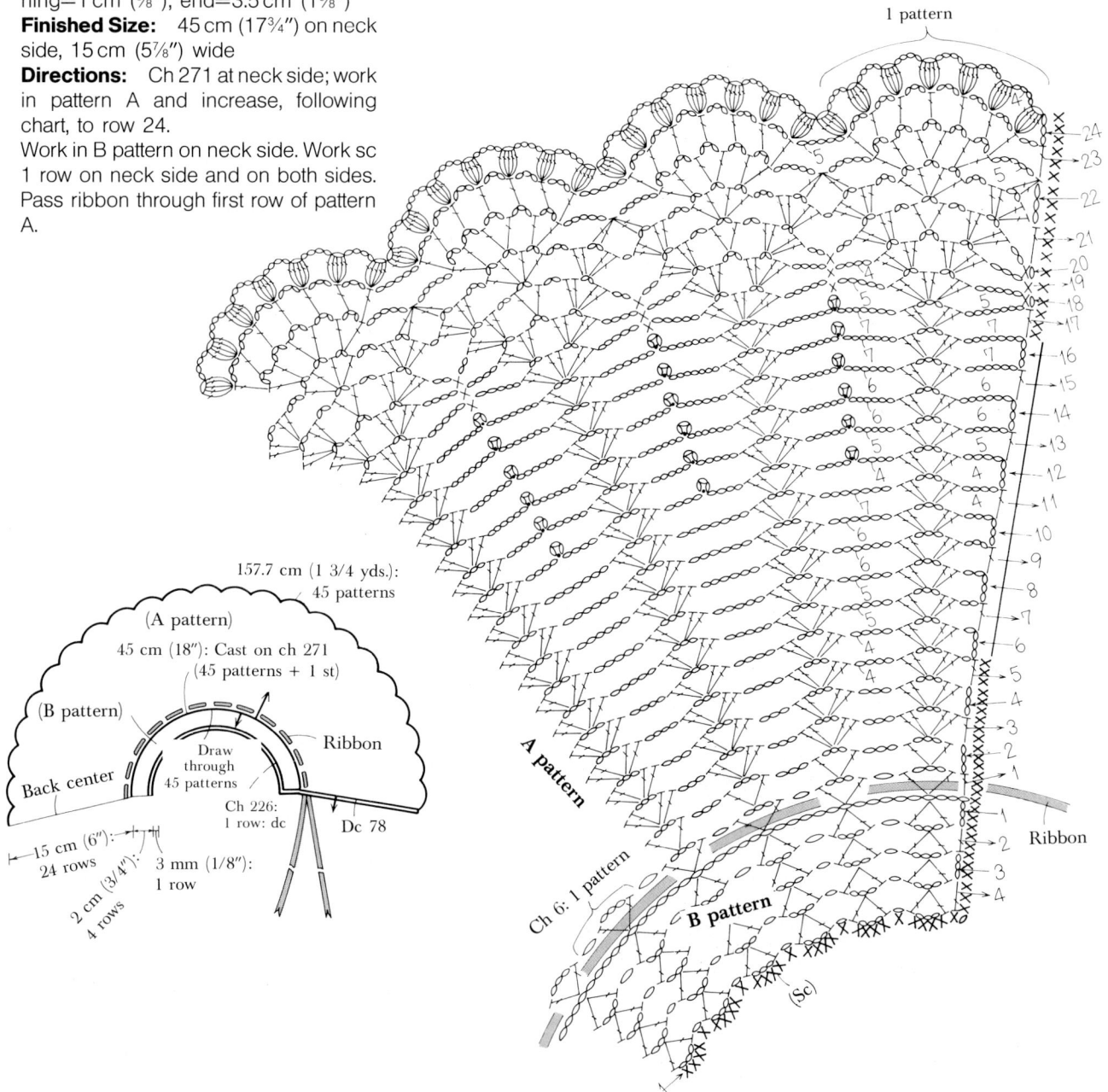

1 pattern

157.7 cm (1 3/4 yds.): 45 patterns

(A pattern)
45 cm (18″): Cast on ch 271 (45 patterns + 1 st)

(B pattern)

Back center

Draw through 45 patterns

Ribbon

Ch 226: 1 row: dc

Dc 78

15 cm (6″): 24 rows

2 cm (3/4″): 4 rows

3 mm (1/8″): 1 row

A pattern

B pattern

Ch 6: 1 pattern

(Sc)

Ribbon

24
23
22
21
20
19
18
17
16
15
14
13
12
11
10
9
8
7
6
5
4
3
2
1

81

39 Pochette

Materials: Anchor Mercer-Crochet no. 30 white, 10 g
Steel crochet hook no. 8 (size 0.9 mm); 35×23 cm (14×9″) black corduroy; 35×17 cm (14×7″) wine red fabric for lining; 180 cm (72″)-length black braid; 2 cm (¾″) black magic tape; some chemical wad; various beads.
Finished Size: 15×17 cm (6×6¾″)

Directions: Cut corduroy and lining, adding 1 cm seam allowance.

Attach crocheted cords, flowers, leaves, and beads on front, following diagram. Sew corduroy and lining separately and make bags. Open side, place lining 3 cm (1¼″) in from edge and slip stitch; attach magic tape 1 cm (⅜″) in from edge. Sew braid on both sides of pochette.

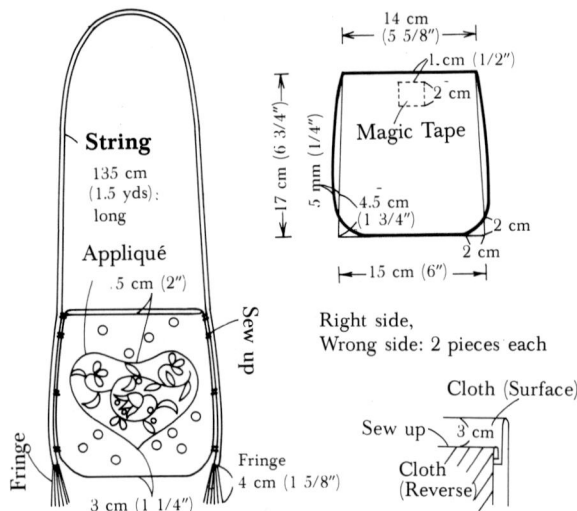

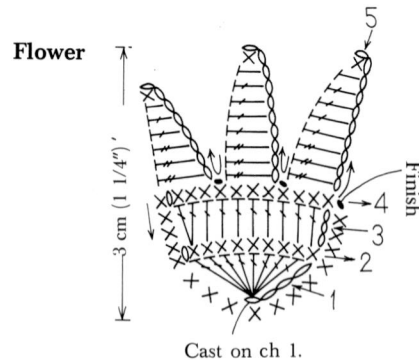

String
135 cm (1.5 yds) long

Appliqué
5 cm (2″)

Sew up

Fringe

Fringe 4 cm (1 5/8″)

3 cm (1 1/4″)

14 cm (5 5/8″)
1 cm (1/2″)
2 cm
Magic Tape
17 cm (6 3/4″)
5 mm (1/4″)
4.5 cm (1 3/4″)
2 cm
2 cm
15 cm (6″)

Right side, Wrong side: 2 pieces each

Cloth (Surface)
Sew up 3 cm
Cloth (Reverse)

Flower
5
4
3
2
Finish
1
3 cm (1 1/4″)
Cast on ch 1.

Leaf

A
Cast on ch 12.
2 cm (3/4″)

B
Cast on ch 10.

C (2 pieces)
Cast on ch 8.
1.5 cm (5/8″)

D
Cast on ch 9.

E
Cast on ch 7.

F
Cast on ch 6.

G
Cast on ch 8.

H
Cast on ch 11.

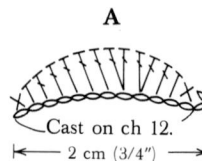

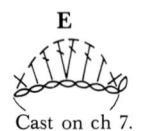

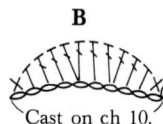

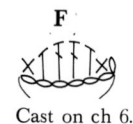

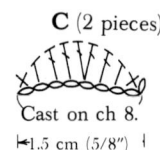

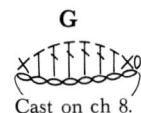

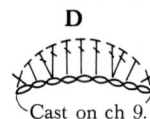

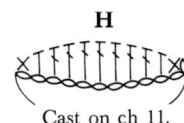

Appliqué Pattern Chart

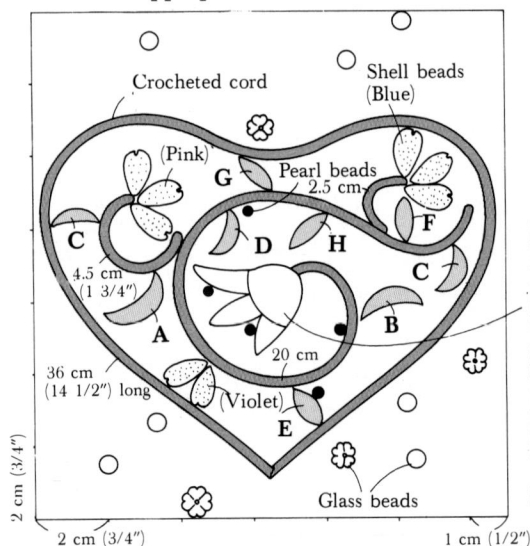

Crocheted cord
Shell beads (Blue)
(Pink)
Pearl beads 2.5 cm
G
C
4.5 cm (1 3/4″)
A
D
H
F
C
B
36 cm (14 1/2″) long
20 cm
(Violet)
E
Glass beads
2 cm (3/4″)
2 cm (3/4″)
1 cm (1/2″)
Flower: Stuff with chemical wad

Mesh Pattern,
Double Crochet,
Breughel lace,
Single Crochet,
Ribbed Stitch,
Pineapple Pattern,
Irish Lace and Flowers

Mesh Pattern

Floral Sampler

How to work the letters:

Materials: Anchor Mercer-Crochet no. 30—60 g (387), some each of light pink, yellow, pale green, blue, lavender, pink, orange, and violet.
Steel crochet hook #8 (size 0.9 mm)
Directions: Follow the chart. The letters should be beige, and the small flowers the colors indicated. The leaf should turn out, with the thread attached to the position on the stem specified.

The chain stitch is like a net; its other name is the wave pattern. The basic mesh pattern is made by repeating 5 chain stitches and 1 single crochet. If one chain is 3 stitches, it will be a small mesh; if there are 7–9 stitches in one chain, it will be the big mesh pattern.

The key to the mesh pattern

- Make all the chain stitches the same size.
- The single crochet should be tight, and when worked, should be like pulling the left-hand thread—the result should be perfectly neat.
- The first chain stitches will be 2 stitches less than one chain, and the result completely flat.

How to increase or decrease the chain stitch when working around or across:

- **In working around:**
  There are two ways to decrease when working around—either slip stitch to the center of the chain, or work up the chain and do double crochet, following chart.
  How to increase:
  There are two ways to increase: one is to increase at the same time as increasing the chain stitches; the other is to increase the mesh of the chain, following chart.
- **In working across:**
  How to increase:
  Follow chart.
  How to decrease:
  Crochet two chains together to decrease the number of chain stitches.

Mesh pattern with picots:
Picots in the applied mesh pattern make the pattern beautiful.

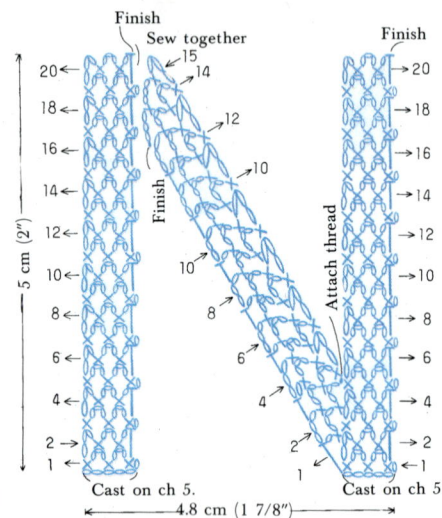

Basic Pattern in Mesh

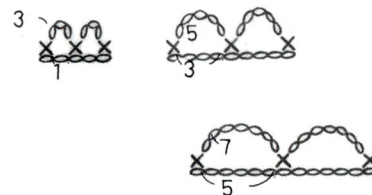

Across

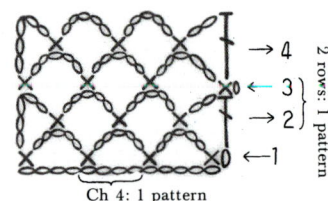

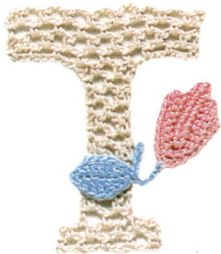

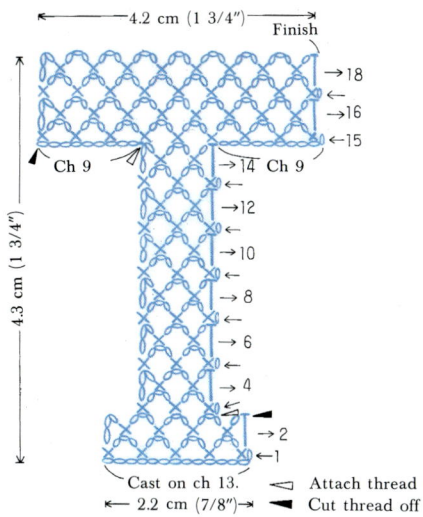

- 4.2 cm (1 3/4")
- Finish
- →18
- ←16
- →16
- ←15
- Ch 9
- ←14 Ch 9
- →12
- ←10
- →8
- ←6
- →4
- →2
- ←1
- 4.3 cm (1 3/4")
- Cast on ch 13.
- 2.2 cm (7/8")
- ▷ Attach thread
- ◀ Cut thread off

With Picots

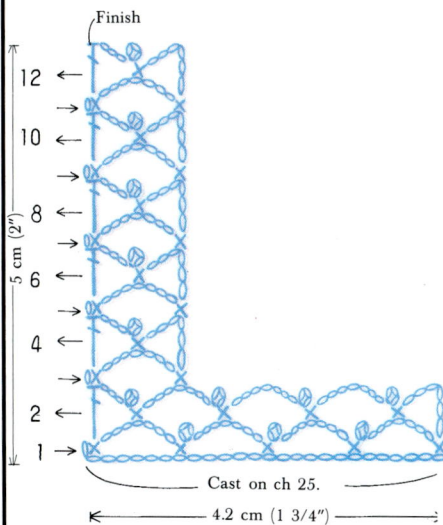

- Finish
- 12 ←
- 10 ←
- 8 →
- 6 ←
- 4 ←
- 2 ←
- 1 →
- 5 cm (2")
- Cast on ch 25.
- 4.2 cm (1 3/4")

With Picots

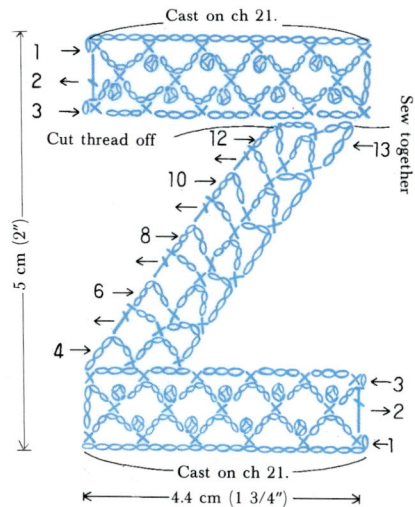

- Cast on ch 21.
- 1 →
- 2 ←
- 3 →
- Cut thread off
- 12 →
- 13 ←
- Sew together
- 10 →
- 8 →
- 6 →
- 4 →
- 3 →
- 2 →
- 1 →
- 5 cm (2")
- Cast on ch 21.
- 4.4 cm (1 3/4")

How to Increase

- Dc
- 5
- 5
- 5
- Ch 3

How to work around

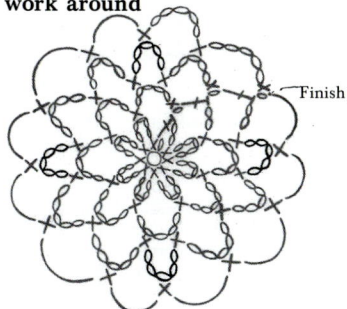

- Finish

Variations of Mesh Pattern with Picots

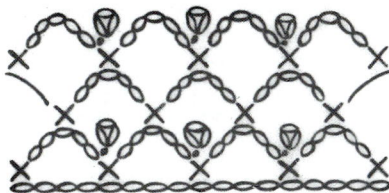

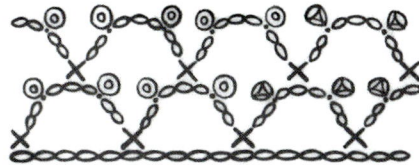

Filet Mesh Pattern/Double Crochet

The filet mesh pattern, which is shaped like a square, is called a square, mesh, or filet pattern. It is made up of double crochet and chain stitches. Work the design in double crochet, and fill in the squares for various other designs.

Basic Filet Mesh Pattern
Follow the chart for basic one-square stitches.

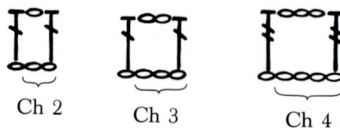

Special Points to Remember
- Make all the stitches the same size for a uniform chain and to keep the work neat. At the double crochet part of the design, pull the top of the double crochet.
- Keep a good balance, the main point of double crochet; #40 crochet cotton is best for this work.
  When one double crochet and 2 chain stitches make one square, the right square's figure is the best.
- When making the structure of the design, a short double crochet in the square space is better than a double crochet in filling out the square.

How to increase and decrease:
As a rule, increase or decrease by the unit of one square. One other way of decreasing is by slip stitches.

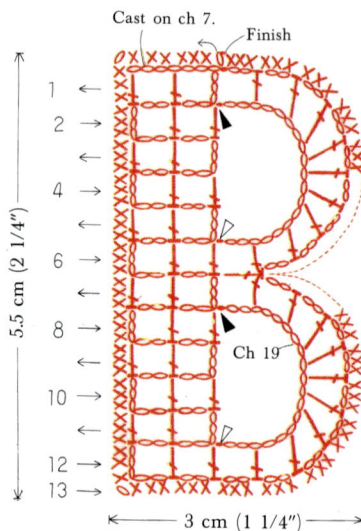

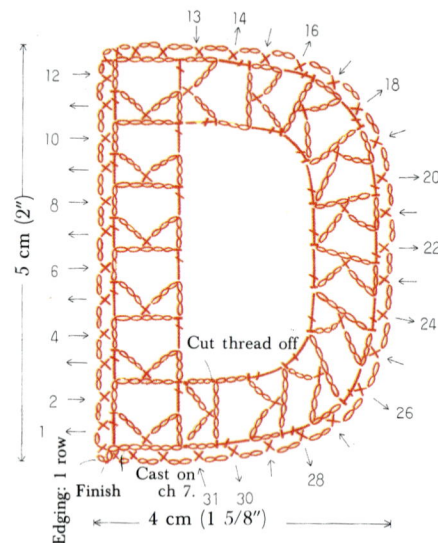

Cast on ch 7. Finish

5.5 cm (2 1/4")

Ch 19

3 cm (1 1/4")

13 14 16 18
20
22
24
26
28

5 cm (2")

Cut thread off

Edging; 1 row

Cast on ch 7. Finish 31 30

4 cm (1 5/8")

Basic One-Square Stitches

Ch 2   Ch 3   Ch 4

How to Increase or Decrease:

Increase at finishing   Increase at beginning

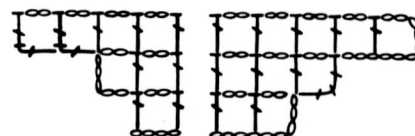

Decrease at finishing   Decrease at beginning

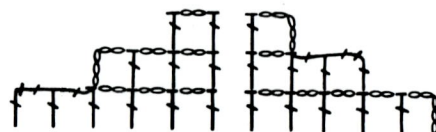

P — 5.3 cm (2 1/4")
Ch 26
Finish
Cast on ch 13.
4 cm (1 5/8")

C — 5.3 cm (2 1/4")
Finish
Cast on ch 35.
3.6 cm (1 1/2")

K — 4.8 cm (2")
Cast on ch 6.
Finish
4 cm (1 5/8")

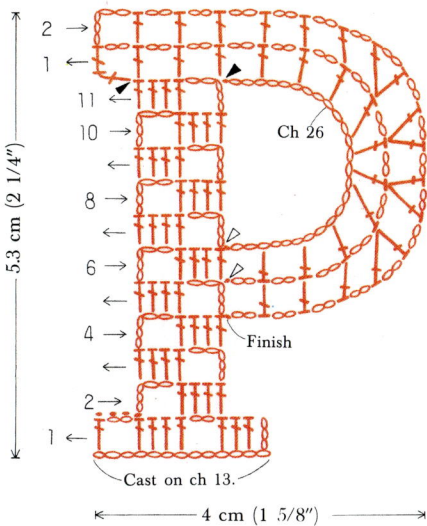

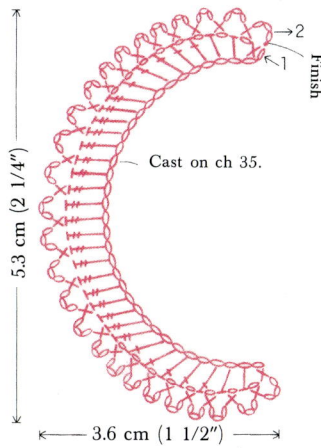

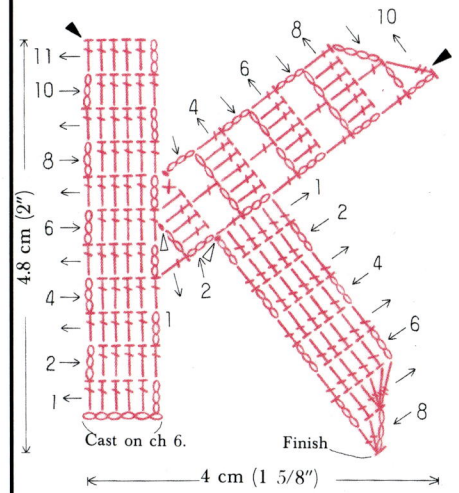

◁ Attach thread
◀ Cut thread off

4 Variations of Filet Mesh Pattern

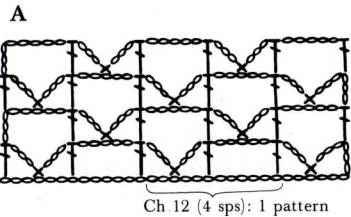

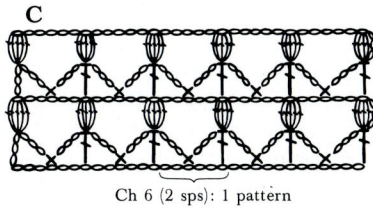

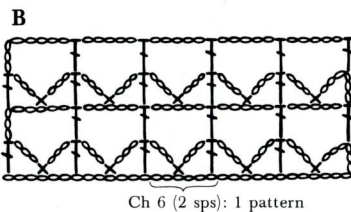

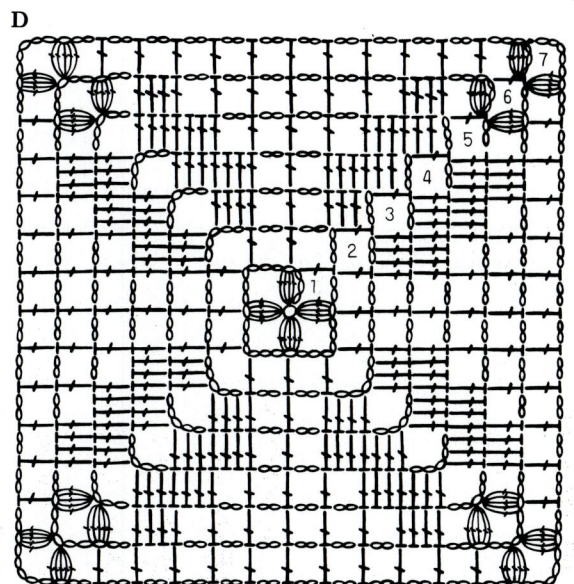

A

Ch 12 (4 sps): 1 pattern

B

Ch 6 (2 sps): 1 pattern

C

Ch 6 (2 sps): 1 pattern

D

Breughel Lace

Breughel lace is also called bogen or band lace. While crocheting the braid you can put together a variety of figures. Breughel is turned smoothly, like a *bogen* or arc in German. It is a simple way to make gorgeous materials.

It is possible to make the figure in a circular, 'S' or 'U' shape, and so make doilies, table centers, shawls, and other accessories.

Basic Braid
Make 4–5 double crochet.
To change from right side to wrong side, make a loop of the chain and then change direction.

Variations of Braid
A: This is called "muddle through," and feels much lighter than the basic pattern.
B: This distinctive technique is at the start, and wide.
C: Put 3 squares in the blank.

How to connect braids
On a curve: After 2 chain stitches, pass crochet hook through 3 loops, pull out thread, slip 1 stitch at once, and work 2 stitches. The shape of the curve depends on the number of loops connected.

In the S sample: After completing 9 rows, work 2 ch st and pass crochet hook through loop of rows 8, 6, and 4. Pull out thread, work one sl st first, and then work 2 ch st. It should be completed in 1 loop. To complete the S sample, work the opposite side's loop on row 18.

Put together 2 braids with double crochet
While working braid, work double or treble crochet in loop of other braid. When it is connected, work 2 chain stitches, put the hook into loop of the other braid, work double or treble crochet and 2 chain stitches, and make braid.

Making ring to connect beginning and end of braid
A: One way to form a ring is by pulling up each stitch. For example, when double crochet is not finished (2 threads on needle), put the hook in the first row and pull together once.
B: After last row, connect as if sewing the beginning and end stitches.
C: The same as B: after last row, connect the beginning and end with a working slip stitch.

Basic Braid

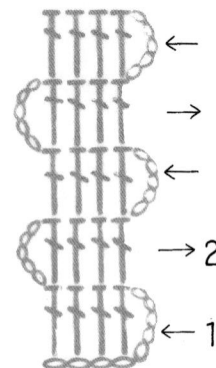

Put together 2 braids with double crochet

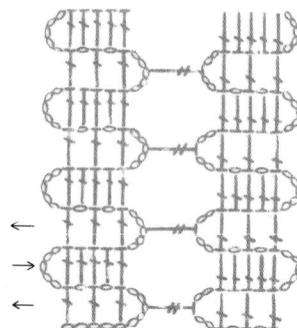

Connect beginning and end of braid

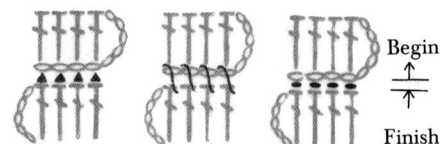

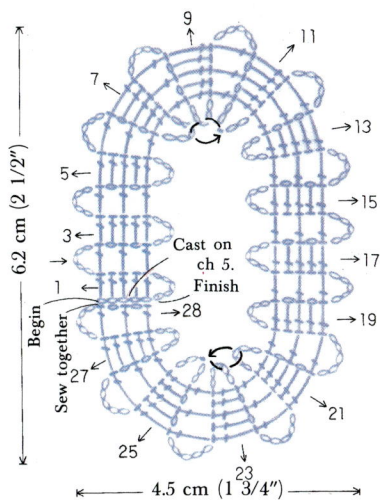

9

11

7

5

13

3

15

Cast on ch 5. Finish

17

Begin

1

28

19

27

Sew together

25

23

21

6.2 cm (2 1/2")

4.5 cm (1 3/4")

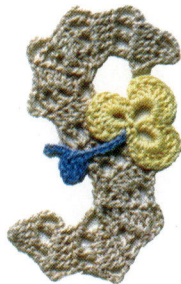

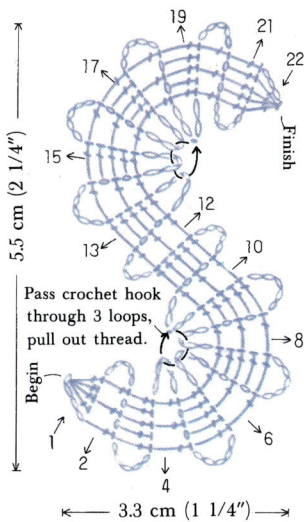

19

21

17

22

Finish

15

12

13

10

Pass crochet hook through 3 loops, pull out thread.

8

Begin

1

2

6

4

5.5 cm (2 1/4")

3.3 cm (1 1/4")

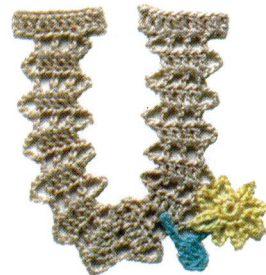

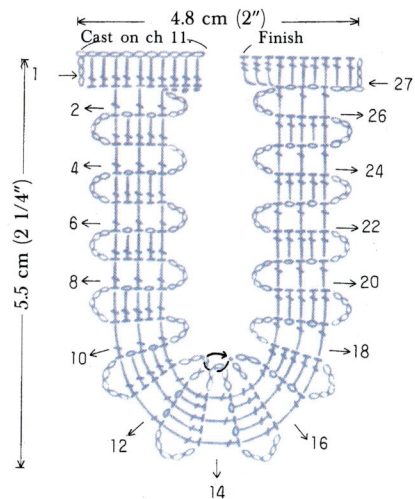

4.8 cm (2")

Cast on ch 11

Finish

1

27

2

26

4

24

6

22

8

20

10

18

12

16

14

5.5 cm (2 1/4")

On a curve

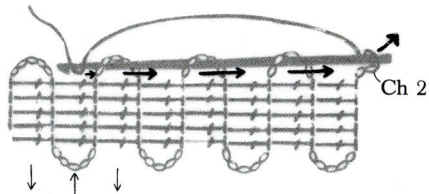

Ch 2

Variations of Braid

A

2

1

B

2

1

C

2

1

Single Crochet/ Ribbed Stitch

Single Crochet

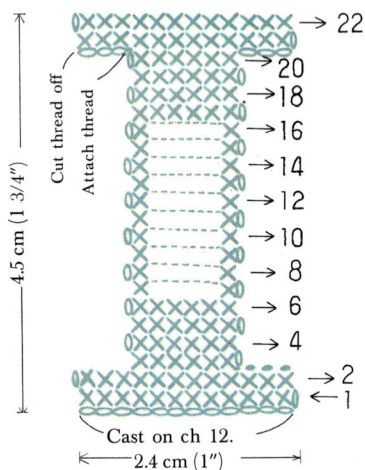

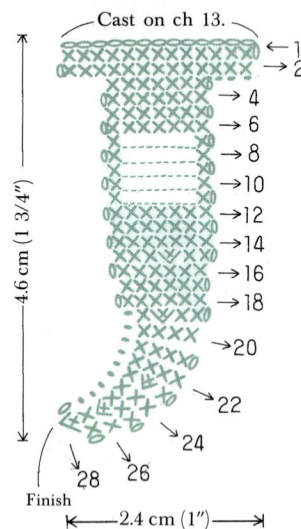

The single crochet is the same size in height and width. One row's height is one chain stitch, but don't count the first as a chain stitch. Beginning with the second row, put the crochet hook into both parts of chain (2 pieces of thread) of the single crochet.

Ribbed Stitch

In the first row, work in regular single crochet.

In the second row, work 1 chain stitch for the rib, put the hook into half a chain (one piece of thread) on the top single crochet of first row, and work single crochet.

Work across, pick up one thread on the other side, and work single crochet every row. The texture is rougher than single crochet.

Single Crochet

→ 22
→ 20
→ 18
→ 16
→ 14
→ 12
→ 10
→ 8
→ 6
→ 4
→ 2
← 1

Cut thread off
Attach thread

4.5 cm (1 3/4")

Cast on ch 12.
← 2.4 cm (1") →

Single Crochet

Cast on ch 13.
← 1
→ 2
→ 4
→ 6
→ 8
→10
→12
→14
→16
→18
→20
→22
→24
28 26

Finish

4.6 cm (1 3/4")

← 2.4 cm (1") →

*Make loop at the end of thread.

Ribbed Stitch

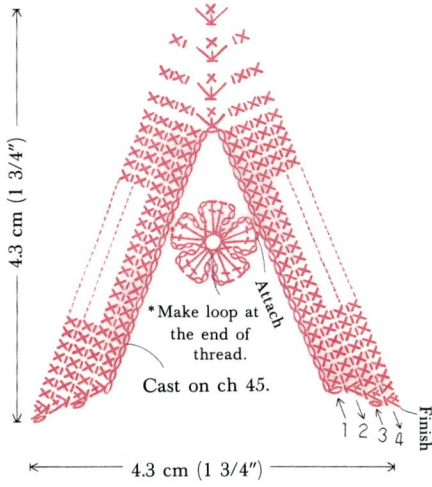

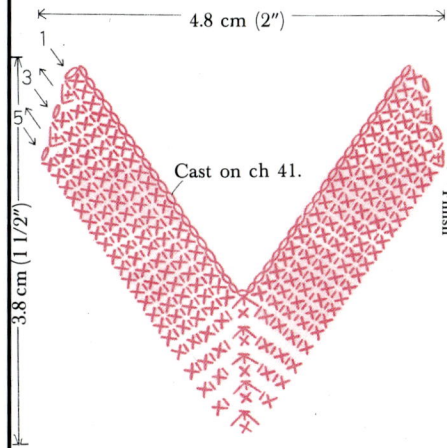

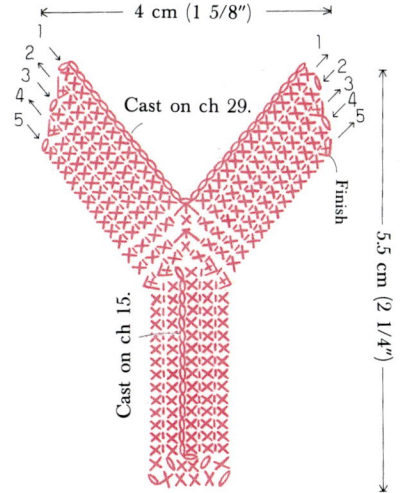

4.3 cm (1 3/4")

4.3 cm (1 3/4")

*Make loop at the end of thread.

Attach

Cast on ch 45.

1 2 3 4 Finish

Ribbed Stitch

4.8 cm (2")

3.8 cm (1 1/2")

1
3
5

Cast on ch 41.

Finish

Ribbed Stitch

4 cm (1 5/8")

5.5 cm (2 1/4")

1
2
3
4
5

Cast on ch 29.

1
2
3
4
5

Finish

Cast on ch 15.

Irish Lace and Small Flowers

This lace was first made in Ireland, in imitation of Venetian point lace, in the latter half of the Middle Ages. The rose—England's national flower—appears frequently as a motif. There are 5-petaled roses, and an easy-to-join 6- or 8-petaled single or double rose and bud. The stem is often worked as an arabesque of leaves with a bunch of grapes.

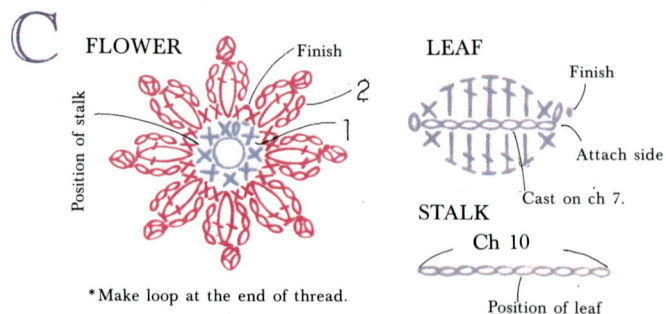

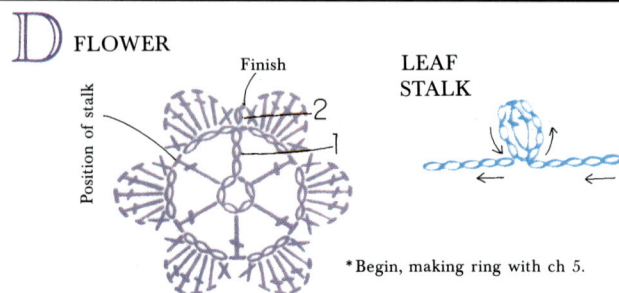

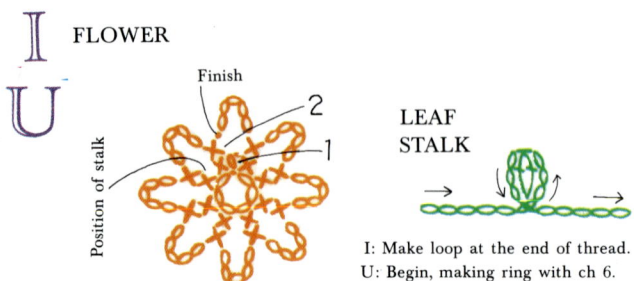

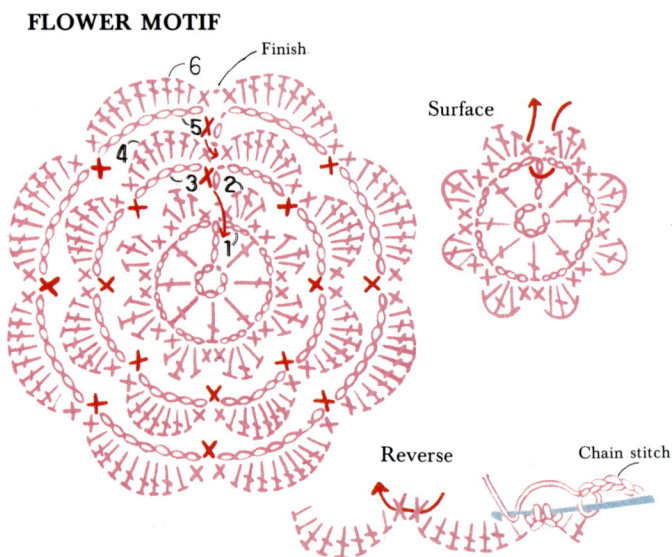

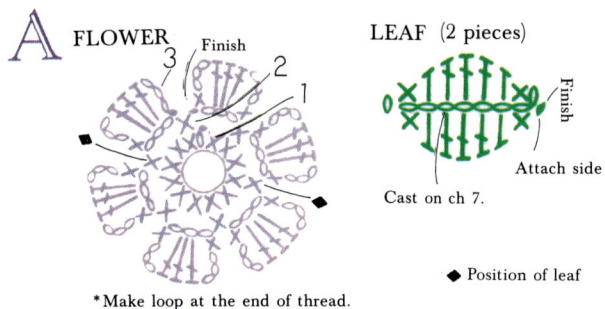

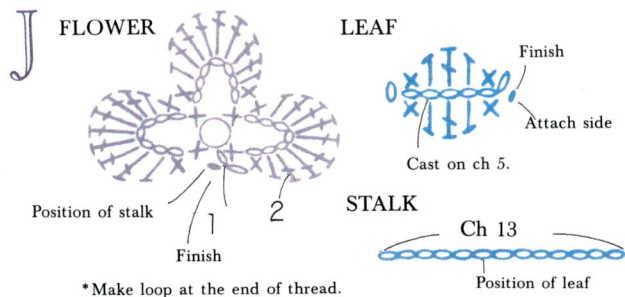

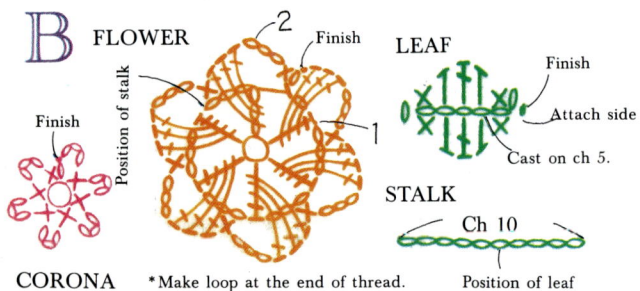

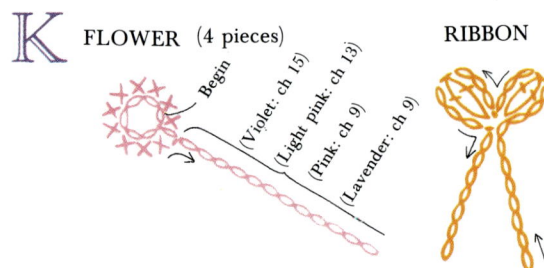

FLOWER MOTIF

6 Finish
5
4
3 2
1

Surface

Reverse

Chain stitch

C
FLOWER
Finish
2
1
Position of stalk

LEAF
Finish
Attach side
Cast on ch 7.

STALK
Ch 10
Position of leaf

*Make loop at the end of thread.

D
FLOWER
Finish
2
1
Position of stalk

LEAF
STALK

*Begin, making ring with ch 5.

I U
FLOWER
Finish
2
1
Position of stalk

LEAF
STALK

I: Make loop at the end of thread.
U: Begin, making ring with ch 6.

A
FLOWER
3 Finish
2
1

LEAF (2 pieces)
Finish
Attach side
Cast on ch 7.

◆ Position of leaf

*Make loop at the end of thread.

J
FLOWER
Position of stalk
Finish
1
2

LEAF
Finish
Attach side
Cast on ch 5.

STALK
Ch 13
Position of leaf

*Make loop at the end of thread.

B
FLOWER
2 Finish
Position of stalk
Finish

LEAF
Finish
Attach side
Cast on ch 5.

STALK
Ch 10
Position of leaf

CORONA

*Make loop at the end of thread.

K
FLOWER (4 pieces)
Begin
(Violet: ch 15)
(Light pink: ch 13)
(Pink: ch 9)
(Lavender: ch 9)

RIBBON

L FLOWER — Finish — 2 — 1 — Position of stalk

LEAF — Finish — Attach side — Cast on ch 7.

STALK — Ch 10 — Position of leaf

T FLOWER — ← 3 — → 2 — ← 1 — → — ◁ — ← — Position of stalk — Cast on ch 8. — Finish

LEAF — Finish — Attach side — Cast on ch 7.

STALK — Ch 10 — Position of leaf

N FLOWER — ← 3 — ← 2 — ← 1 — ← — ← — ← — Position of stalk — Finish — Cast on ch 7.

LEAF STALK — → — →

V FLOWER — Finish — 2 — 1 — Position of stalk

LEAF — Finish — Attach side — Cast on ch 5.

STALK — Ch 15 — Position of leaf

*Begin making ring with ch 6.

O FLOWER (2 pieces) — Finish — (Yellow: ch 10) — (Pink: ch 13)

RIBBON

Y FLOWER — Finish — ② — ③ — ① — Finish — Finish — Position of stalk

STALK — Ch 10 — Position of leaf

LEAF — Finish — Attach side — Cast on ch 5.

P FLOWER — Finish — 2 — 1 — Position of stalk

LEAF STALK

*Begin, making ring with ch 5.

Z FLOWER — Finish — 2 — 1 — Position of stalk

LEAF STALK — → — →

*Make loop at the end of thread.

S FLOWER — Position of stalk — 1 — 2 — Finish

LEAF STALK

*Make loop at the end of thread.

PINEAPPLE FLOWER — 3 — Finish — 2 — 1

SMALL FLOWER — Finish — Position of stalk

LEAF (2 pieces) — Finish — Attach side — Cast on ch 7.

◆ Position of leaf

STALK — Ch 15

*Make loop at the end of thread.

Pineapple Pattern

The pineapple design has been popular for a long time. It can be found on the pottery and fabrics of Persia and India. The mesh part of the pattern is shaped like a pinecone, but the figure is a pineapple.

The Basic Pineapple Pattern

The base, working up to the mesh pattern, is double crochet.

Work one chain less than preceding row. The mesh pattern has as its base a double crochet of 7 st; the first row of the mesh pattern is 5 ch, the second is 4 ch, third is 3 ch, the fourth is 2 ch, and the last is 1 ch. The size of the pattern lace can be changed: shell pattern, double crochet popcorn, double crochet, etc.

The key to the pineapple pattern

- In the pinecone net, the single crochet should be the center of the chain of the preceding row.
- The pinecone's chain stitches should be very neatly worked.

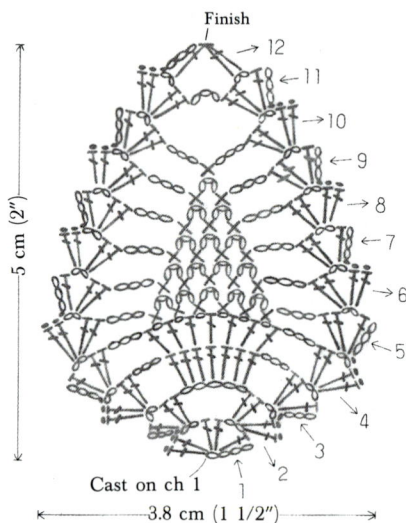

Finish

→ 12
← 11
→ 10
← 9
→ 8
← 7
→ 6
← 5
→ 4
3
↑ 2
1

5 cm (2")

Cast on ch 1

3.8 cm (1 1/2")

The Basic Pineapple Pattern

Foundation of dc 9 st.

Variations of Pineapple Pattern

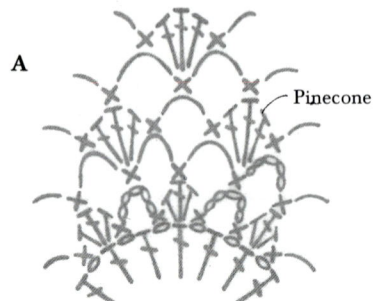

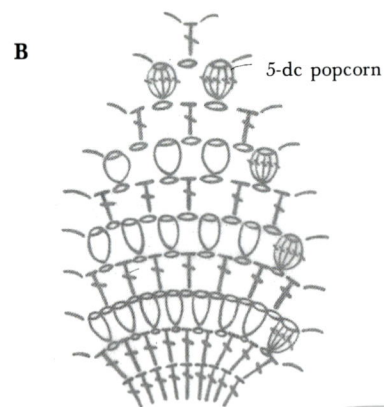

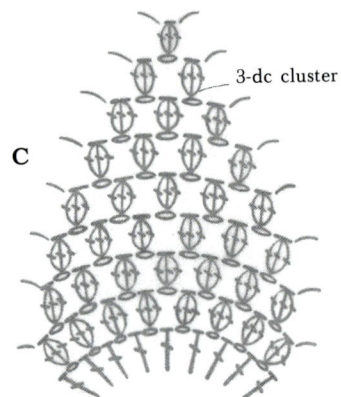

A

Pinecone

B

5-dc popcorn

C

3-dc cluster

The Basics of Crochet

Chain stitch (ch)

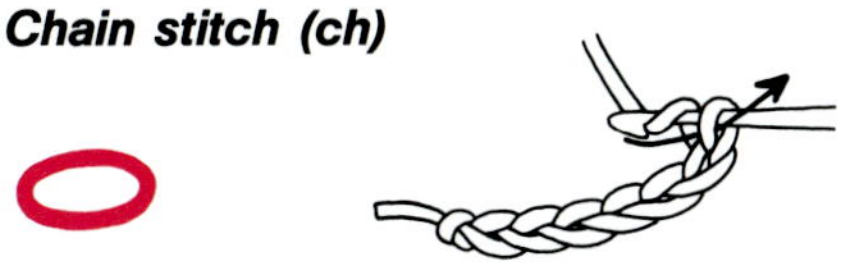

Slip stitch (sl st)

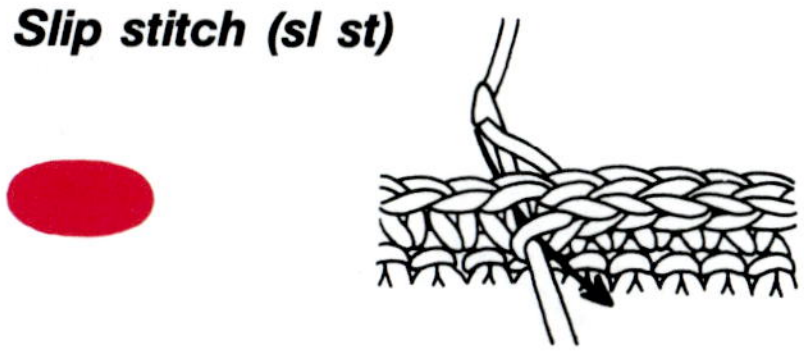

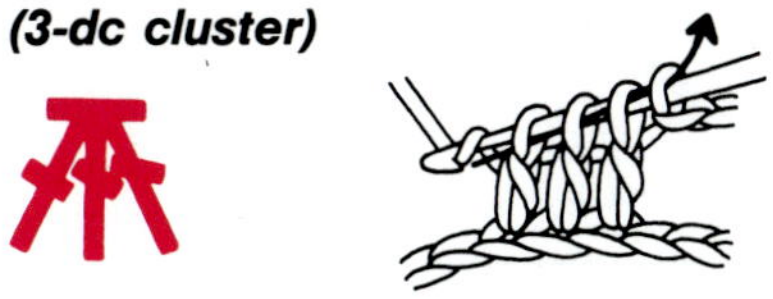

2 half double crochet increase (2-hdc inc.)

Single Crochet (sc)

Ch 1

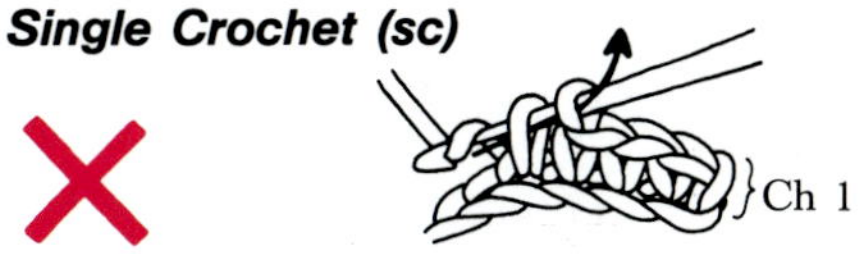

Half double crochet (hdc)

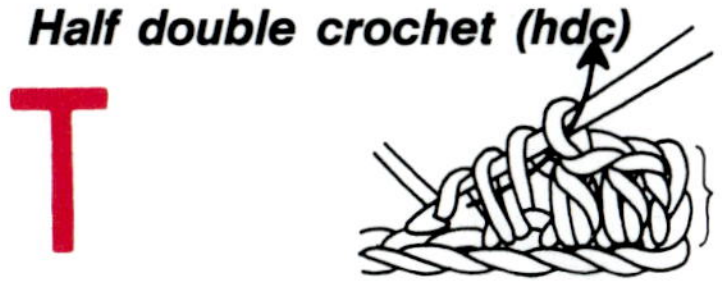

2 single crochet increase (2-sc inc.)

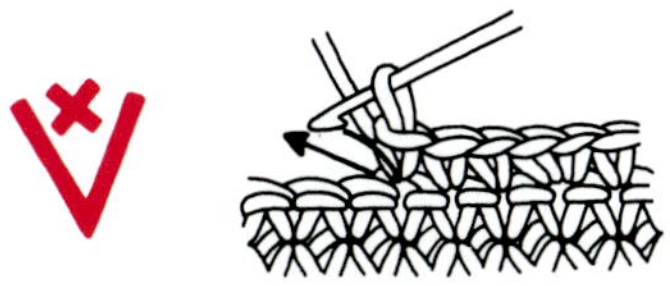

Double crochet (dc)

Ch 3

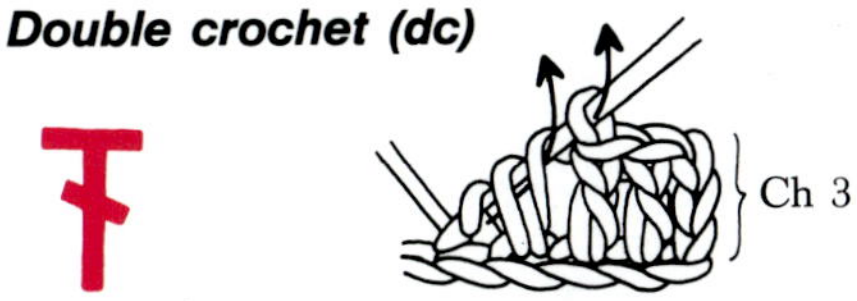

Treble crochet (tr or trc)

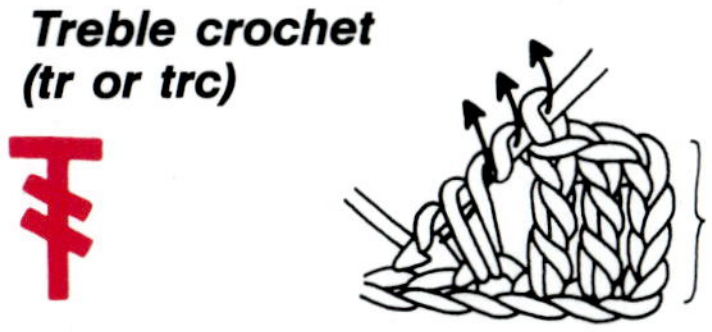

3 single crochet increase (3-sc inc.)

3 Double crochet puff (3-dc puff)

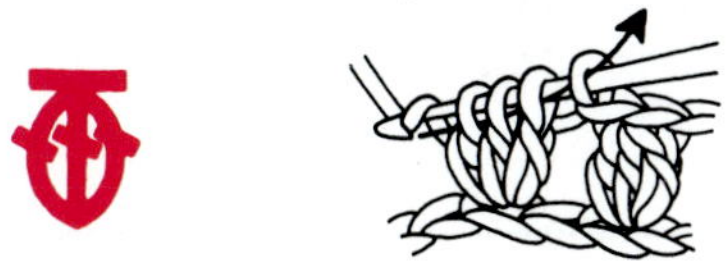

2 half double crochet cluster (2-hdc cluster)

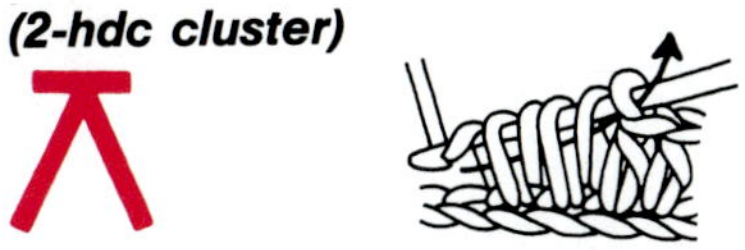

3 half double crochet increase (3-hdc inc.)

4 double crochet popcorn (4-dc popcorn)

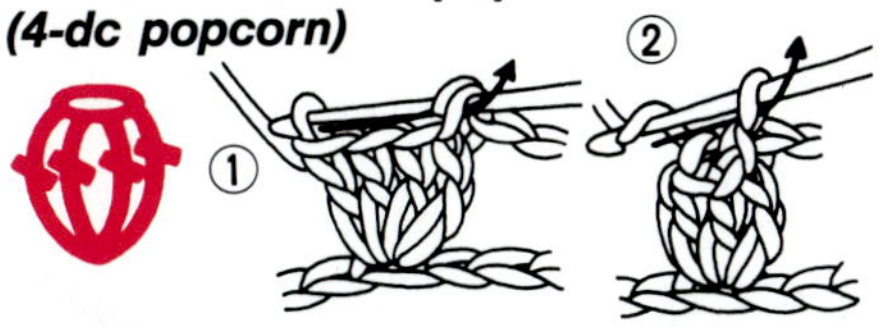

① ②

3 double crochet cluster (3-dc cluster)

4 double crochet increase (4-dc inc.)

Quadruple crochet

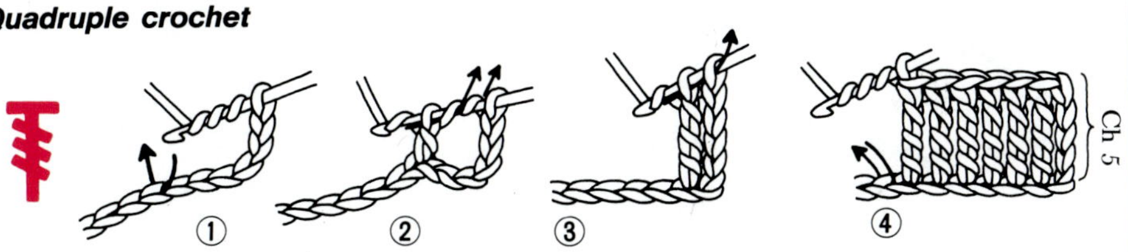

① ② ③ ④

Ch 5

Ribbed stitch

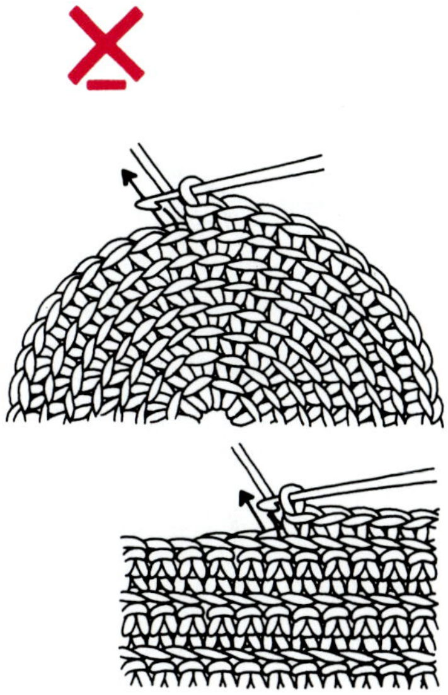

Double crochet cross

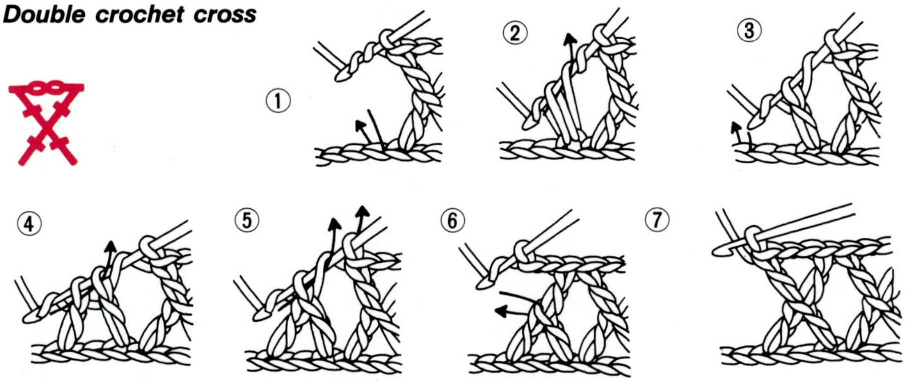

① ② ③

④ ⑤ ⑥ ⑦

To begin: Begin with loop

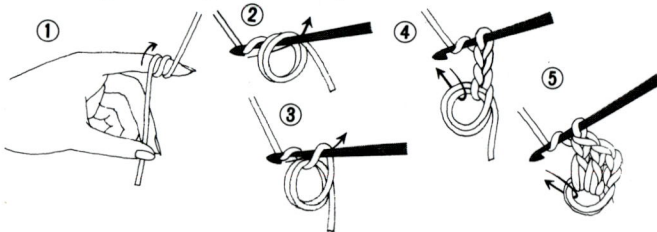

① ② ③ ④ ⑤

Begin with chain to form ring

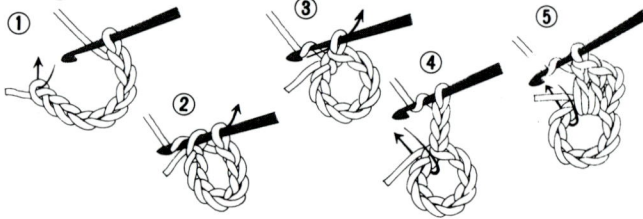

① ② ③ ④ ⑤

Picot: Slip stitch picot

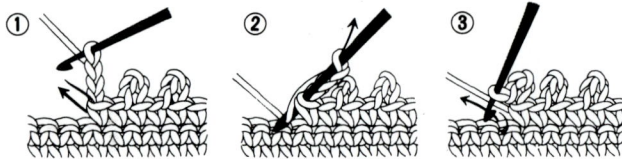

① ② ③

Loop picot

① ②

Crocheted cord

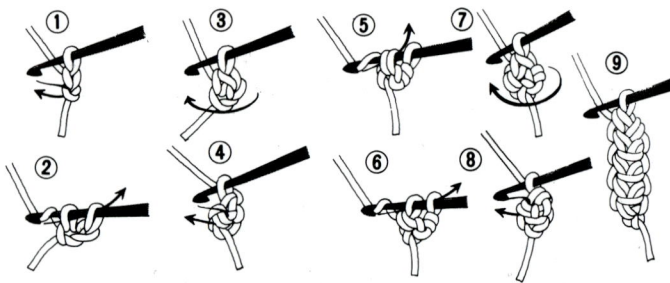

① ② ③ ④ ⑤ ⑥ ⑦ ⑧ ⑨

Spider web stitch

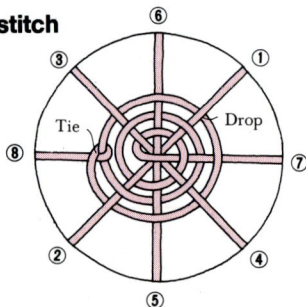

⑥ ③ ① Tie Drop ⑧ ⑦ ② ④ ⑤

Single crochet from left to right

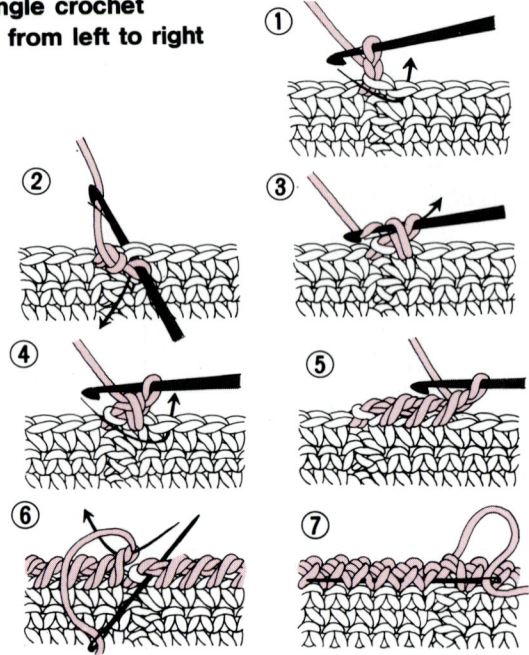

① ② ③ ④ ⑤ ⑥ ⑦

How to connect motifs
Connecting with slip stitch

A: Drop loop from hook in net, pick up dropped loop and pull through net.

B: Insert hook in center stitch of one chain. Pull thread through it.

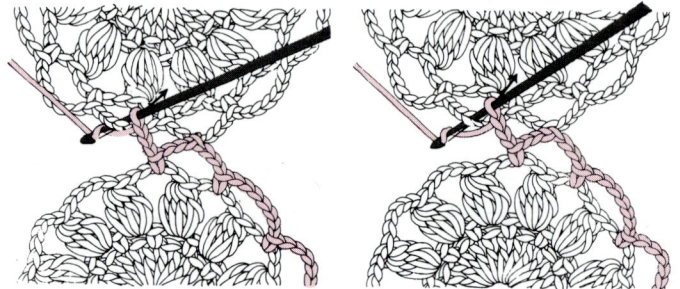

Connecting with single crochet

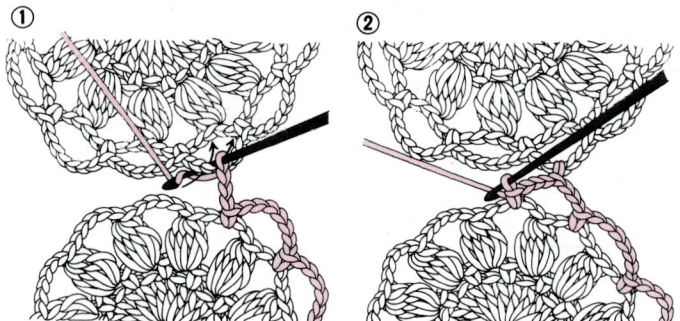

① ②